# Reconciling
## an
# Oppressor

# Reconciling an Oppressor

## MICHAEL V. FARISS

Pleasant Word
A Division of WINEPRESS PUBLISHING

Printed in the United States of America

Packaged by WinePress Publishing, PO Box 428, Enumclaw, WA 98022. The views expressed or implied in this work do not necessarily reflect those of WinePress Publishing. Ultimate design, content, and editorial accuracy of this work are the responsibilities of the author.

Unless otherwise noted, all Scriptures are taken from the King James Version of the Holy Bible.

Verses marked NKJV are taken from the *New King James Version*. Copyright © 1979, 1980, 1982 by Thomas Nelson, Inc. Used by permission. All Rights Reserved.

ISBN 1-57921-536-X
Library of Congress Catalog Card Number: 2002115825

# Table Of Contents

# Preface

At the youth center in Norfolk, VA, where I began to minister full-time to urban young people twenty-two years ago, I often sat in a second-floor windowsill, waiting for students to arrive for our after-school programs. When the day ended at the public high school across the street, I would watch an overwhelming number of them rush to buses that headed out from the school's suburb to their impoverished neighborhoods. Alone while I waited, I asked God to show me how to make a lasting difference in their lives.

I believe God answered these prayers through my desperate search for solutions to problems that destroyed many of these teenagers. *Reconciling an Oppressor* includes a first-hand introduction to young people who suffered while I learned. I changed some of their names and I left others the same; all should know by now that I love them and their families. For those young people who died, I hope that their stories will somehow help others trust Jesus Christ.

I thank every person mentioned in these pages that God used to bless my life. I anticipate that many more faithful persons not recognized here, who stood with me in financial, prayer, and volunteer support, will one day see their investments, given in secret, greatly rewarded by our Lord.

This account of my twenty-two years of inner-city ministry also introduces Urban Discovery Ministries and our vision for inner-city outreach. It celebrates my friendship and ministry with Ken Watson as we pursued racial reconciliation through the gospel. We developed a desire to fulfill the Great Commission of Jesus Christ in a way that unites white and black Christian forces to glorify Him as one people. Ken and I found this reconciliation, which achieved far more than just assimilating African-American into the white Christian mainstream, to make up for past wrongs. Certainly, other Christians in past generations found the same reconciliation by serving in world missions or the abolitionist and civil rights movements, without racially segregating themselves. Although I cannot go back in time to support their causes, I look forward to standing with them before the Lord. I trust that He will say about me: "I reconciled this oppressor."

Michael V. Fariss

# CHAPTER 1

# How Did You Get In Here?

*Newspaper account of drug Crisis in Huntersville Village*

My wife Kim handed me the phone and said, "It's Tito." Concerned because I seldom heard from Tito unless something was wrong, I put down my wrench and took the receiver. This time his words tore into me, "Mike, Chris has been shot. I think he's dead." I froze. Kim gave me a look that said, "Remember, my parents came here to celebrate my birthday; please do not do anything tonight." To make things worse, I stopped installing her birthday present, a new gas stove on which she hoped to cook her special dinner. The stove rested in the middle of the kitchen with tools and instructions perched on it like a workbench. "I've got to go to the Village," I said. "Tito said that Chris was shot and he's dead." I said this as tersely as I could to hide my shock and to prevent discussion or objections.

Kim and her parents knew exactly where I intended to go. The "Village" meant an apartment complex where I found myself in the middle of a spiritual brawl. During our ten years of youth outreach in the Village, we saw our investment in the lives of its residents being destroyed; as if Satan drew a line in the sand there. I believed God allowed this showdown to prove the gospel powerful enough to intervene in the worst urban environment. If we could intervene in the Village, I became certain that we could evangelize inner-city neighborhoods anywhere.

While starting up the ministry in 1980, I appreciated opportunities I had to ask Lem Tucker of Voice of Calvary Ministries for advice when he traveled to Norfolk to visit his relatives. He instructed us on the community development model established by John Perkins in Mississippi and gave me ideas for launching UDM (Urban Discovery Ministries).

I carried out one of his ideas right away by linking up with the Fellowship of Christian Athletes. This national organization gave us the avenue of athletics to reach high school young people from the inner city. I sponsored an FCA "huddle" and established a sports ministry at a local high school. I followed the high school basketball players to a gym where they competed in the off-season. Located in a community center in the neighborhood of Huntersville, the gym stood across the street from the Huntersville Village Apartments, or just the "Village" to its residents.

I played basketball there during "adult nights" once or twice a week, intending to establish relationships with athletes and to share the good news of Jesus Christ. Instead, I encountered a community of boldly immoral young adults who abused marijuana and alcohol. Many played basketball while stoned. Some teenagers even played in their games at school while "high." I soon discovered that the coaches of the youth teams in Huntersville also abused drugs. A volunteer coach ridiculed me when I protested this behavior. These coaches built good teams, but they set their players up for destruction. They acclimated the children to drugs, who then made an easy transition to selling crack when it became available. Many of the young adult pot smokers turned into crack addicts by 1990. They bought drugs from the younger kids whom they had so poorly influenced.

For some reason, the Lord kept me close to this neighborhood. At this juncture, I met Ken Watson, then a juvenile probation officer in Huntersville, who joined forces with me. Ken had played football at the University of Maryland after competing at a high school in Norfolk, and we began reaching out to young people through sports ministries.

During the summers, I worked with Huntersville young people in Bible clubs, open-air meetings, and camps. Twice a year I sponsored and directed retreats at the Triple R Ranch for over 140 urban children each time. I met Tito at one of these retreats. A young leader among his peers, Tito played basketball for one of the drug abusers. He loved our camps, and we grew close. Along with several high school kids from Huntersville who accepted Christ, Tito kept me involved in the Village.

I learned hard lessons about mentoring in the inner city in Huntersville. Initially, I felt intimidated by parents in this environment and would not confront them about their immorality, irresponsibility, and drug abuse. God soon corrected this aspect of my ministry.

Eventually, the recreation department replaced the Huntersville volunteer coaches and discontinued their athletic teams. Tito asked me to coach his team of twelve-year-olds who had been abandoned in the change of leadership. He appealed on my behalf to the new recreation center director, and I suddenly became Coach Mike of the Huntersville Pacers.

Excited about coaching, I decided to scout the players whom I had inherited. Because the recreation center had closed that particular day, I found my team on an outdoor court at a boarded-up school in Huntersville. I sat in my car and prayed for God's help and wisdom to coach and reach them. One young teen stood out to me because of his potential. A little taller than the rest, he had big hands at the end of long, gangly arms. I noticed that he drove hard to the basket almost every time he received the ball. I thought, *I am going to work with this kid and play him at the point guard position. With his height, he might become a college prospect someday.* I found out that his name was Chris McGlone.

Chris's achievements took us to the recreation league basketball championship in my first year. I constantly challenged him to develop difficult skills. Our relationship grew strong as he succeeded in mastering them. We also established a spiritual bond during the season. He lived in a large neighborhood behind the recreation center and opposite the Village, so I had a special Bible study with him in his apartment. His close friend, Tom, would come and lead the singing. One afternoon, as we sat together in the gymnasium, I introduced Chris to Jesus Christ.

I remember tossing around a football with Chris and Tito in a large field next to the recreation center. When it became dark, we sat down in the grass to talk and pray. Both asked God to save their mothers. We did not realize the ramifications of this intercession as the neighborhood moved into a spiritual and moral crisis. This crisis took Chris's life and spawned UDM's church-planting ministry through Tito's mom, Brenda.

In the spring of 1990, I drove past the Huntersville Village Apartments with my daughter, Rebekah, who was six at the time, and my four-year-old son, Brent. For some reason, I decided to stop at Tito's apartment to set up a time for us to get together. Dropping in on his mom, Brenda, always proved interesting. At age fourteen when Tito was born, she dropped out of school and had two more sons. The man whom she lived with for twenty years had recently died of a heroin overdose. Brenda was thin because she constantly smoked marijuana, which ruined her appetite for food. Sometimes her supplier, whom she called, "dope man," would sit in her apartment when I visited. He portrayed himself as a Jamaican Rastafarian who specialized in organizing pot parties.

Occasionally, I would try to visit Brenda with Gina Miller, our staff member who discipled teenage girls. Brenda worked hard to duck us by going out the back door to avoid our witness. Unlike her sister, "Shell," who gave me some of the meanest looks of anyone in Huntersville, Brenda acted friendly when we managed to catch up with her.

On this visit, I planned to ask for Tito. I parked in front of their apartment so that I could leave my children in the car. When I opened the car door, I sensed something wrong in the neighborhood. I felt tension or maybe an evil presence there. A woman passed me with an angry stare. A young man walked by and yelled unnecessarily loud, "Hey Mike!" I could tell that he had signaled to someone that he knew me. When I entered Brenda's apartment, she peeked through her blinds and asked me, "How did you get in here?" I realized that I had pulled up into a dangerous situation. After a few words with Brenda about Tito, I rushed back to my children and took off in our car.

At the edge of the parking lot, I saw other players from my basketball team riding their bikes up and down the sidewalk. When they saw me, they looked embarrassed. They reacted as if I had caught them doing something wrong. I said to myself, "What I've heard is true. These kids are helping the older guys sell drugs." That realization deeply hurt me.

Two days later, the television news announced a big drug raid in the same parking lot. From a vacant apartment, two police officers had videotaped the drug market there. They recorded over one hundred drug sales in the lot. The evening news played the police videos showing drug dealers using small children as their drug carriers. The dealers hid cocaine in the children's pants and sent them on deliveries. The police raided the neighborhood after the drug dealers noticed the video camera and broke down the door to the apartment where it was hidden. A young man boldly entered the apartment and began shooting until police returned fire and chased him away.

The police designated the neighborhood as the worst drug problem in the city. The assistant city manager called a neighborhood town hall meeting in the community center to discuss how to solve the crisis. I decided to attend and took a seat near the back. A lieutenant began making a presentation to the crowd that filled the room. When the officer finished his talk, he opened the meeting for questions. A man with dreadlocks started shouting accusations of police brutality. He told of officers beating up teenagers and dogs nearly attacking small children. I knew him from several years before when he, stoned, would come to the Discovery Center during the last bell of the school day. He spoke now as a leader in the Village's drug trade.

In support of this young man's argument, an angry group of residents broke out in loud debate against the police. A detective justified the police's rough treatment by holding up a black Uzi machine gun that he had confiscated from a young person in the neighborhood. The detective said that the gun was deadly enough to fire twenty-two rounds in the time that it took for a police officer to fire once. I felt uneasy, since this confrontation escalated between the exit and where I sat. Finally, the man with the dreadlocks stomped out while cursing the authorities out loud. The angry group followed him out. What happened next caught me off guard.

The young people of the neighborhood, many of whom I had coached, taken to camp, or tried to mentor, marched out defiantly in support of the drug dealer. After catching up with Tito, I attempted to talk him out of this evil. We caught the downtown ferry to the other side of the Elizabeth River and sat on the boardwalk to talk. I offered him all the help and support I possibly could give him. I warned him of the consequences of drugs. Though I begged him to stop and tried to reason with him from the Scriptures, he coldly turned me down. The drug dealers had successfully recruited him. His natural leadership ability boosted him up their conspiracy's ladder.

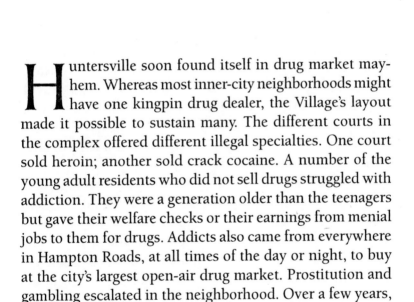

# CHAPTER 2

# The Huntersville Posse

Huntersville soon found itself in drug market mayhem. Whereas most inner-city neighborhoods might have one kingpin drug dealer, the Village's layout made it possible to sustain many. The different courts in the complex offered different illegal specialties. One court sold heroin; another sold crack cocaine. A number of the young adult residents who did not sell drugs struggled with addiction. They were a generation older than the teenagers but gave their welfare checks or their earnings from menial jobs to them for drugs. Addicts also came from everywhere in Hampton Roads, at all times of the day or night, to buy at the city's largest open-air drug market. Prostitution and gambling escalated in the neighborhood. Over a few years, millions of dollars passed to the drug dealers.

Initially, instant success and money exhilarated the young men who sold drugs. They became overnight sensations. At first, no negative consequences seemed to threaten the young people for selling drugs. They operated like innocent kids in the neighborhood, not vicious killers. As friends, they sold to older people who had abused drugs since these teens could remember. The young people took the business that came to them and did not attempt to hook anyone on drugs. Many of the leaders of the drug trade earned respect from their peers as former high school athletes. They spent many hours in the recreation center displaying their athletic skills. Now with drug money, they became heroes in the neighborhood. They drove beautiful BMWs. Sometimes they even helped people in need. One young man carried a stack of bills in his hand as he walked through the community. He often gave to children who requested money.

Teenagers who once relied on free lunches now enjoyed the lifestyle of corporate executives. They called taxies when they wanted to go to the mall. For the first times in their lives they could afford to eat out and order expensive meals. They stayed in hotels. The drug dealers worked all night long and slept through the day. They became consumers, buying 14-karat gold, Starter jackets, and the latest basketball shoes. Teenage girls and even older women pursued these guys relentlessly.

The drug dealers developed their own theology and government. By merging the teachings of several religions with racist beliefs from the Nation of Islam, the young men found reasons to hold others responsible for their need to sell drugs. They blamed the police, the white establishment, the white conspirators who brought the drugs into the country, and the lack of an alternative means of survival. These young people assumed that they could reasonably reject our government's laws because of the injustices they experienced. The neighborhood's layout made it easy for them to operate in their own little world. Those selling drugs set up their own street code of ethics, which gave them a false sense of integrity and security.

The young people organized under the gang name, "the Huntersville Posse," and promoted their logo, "HVP," in graffiti on the walls and sidewalks of the Village. The bad example of a former athlete motivated them. Only twenty years old, he used drug money to buy cars, a home in the suburbs, and several businesses. He even attended college to achieve his goal of coaching high school football. Most of all, the hurt and hopelessness that the kids felt fueled the expanding drug trade. Instant gratification from drug money appeased their anger.

Tito dumped me to hustle drugs with this gang in the Village. I heard that he decided to drop out of school one morning while smoking marijuana with his friends at the bus stop. They concluded that their new careers in drugs made attending school an unnecessary hassle. The gang dropped out of school together on the same day.

For safety reasons, I decided to avoid the Village. I remember sitting at the traffic light outside the community. There I could see the police raiding an apartment in the Village's cocaine court. I prayed, "God, what kind of missionary am I? You sent me to the Huntersville Village but now I cannot even walk in the neighborhood. Out of all the places in Norfolk, the neighborhood that You called me to reach is the worst in the city. Satan has shut me down. You've got to do something." Little did I know that the apartment busted by the police would soon become my avenue to intervene in the Village's cocaine court. God also answered this request by giving distinctive strategies on which we built Urban Discovery Ministries and our community outreach model.

# CHAPTER 3

# I Never Heard
# It This Way

T hrough the power of the gospel, all believers in Jesus Christ have the potential to minister across racial lines and cultural barriers, including effective outreach in the inner city. I learned this lesson from John Peoples during my first year as an urban missionary in Norfolk, Virginia.

At the age of twenty-three, I directed the Tabernacle Church of Norfolk's Discovery Youth Center, which later the church incorporated as Urban Discovery Ministries. Black teenagers, bused to the high school located across the street from our center, attended our after-school program. To reach their families, my wife, Kim, and I joined Faith Community Church in the Park Place neighborhood, where many of these students lived.

Through the Discovery Youth Center, I tried to reach out to a teenager named Alford, a strong-willed but likable ninth grader. He needed a job for his distributive education class, so I hired him to clean our center. Since Alford appreciated my help and worked diligently, I became concerned when he stopped coming after school. I called his mother and she asked for my help with a family crisis. Alford had moved in with his bedridden uncle and aunt to watch over them. His mother confided to me her fear that the aunt and uncle's house might blow up with Alford inside.

I did not have anyone to take with me to visit them, so I ventured out alone into the December night. I found myself standing in the dark on Alford's uncle's sagging porch, facing a dark blue house, which seemed to sink into the ground on one side. The house, subdivided into two apartments, forced me to choose between two possible entrances, a pitch-dark stairway to the second floor or the broken door in front of me. I stepped back to look at the blue, tilting slum house. Since I feared the danger of the stairway, I banged on the broken door.

A young white man, alone and knocking at night in this impoverished urban neighborhood, I tried to imagine the response of the persons inside the house. Someone tersely yelled, "Who is it?" I felt strange yelling back, "Mike! Alford's friend." Peering through the small window in the door, I saw a hand take hold of a large, thick bolt and pull it out of a latch to unlock the door. Alford's mother welcomed me into a cluttered, dimly lit dwelling. Walking at a sharp slant, she led me to a portable cot in what should have been the dining room. Alford's aunt, Mrs. Peoples, lay semi-conscious on the cot, wrapped up in white sheets. Lumber scraps lay piled up from her bed to a nearby antique wood stove. A large crack ran down the stove's cast iron side, through which I could see a blazing fire. Occasionally, when the fire popped, dangerous sparks shot through the crack and drifted across the room.

I continued to walk past her bed and glanced into a bathroom. The sight of a sink, toilet, and bathtub, blackened by coal which someone stored there, shocked me. In the back room, I met Mr. Peoples. A huge cast covered his leg because he broke it badly when he wrecked his moped.

Though in his late sixties, Mr. Peoples was big and heavy, a strong-looking, gruff man. Unshaven and bedridden, he looked downtrodden. In his dark room, he wore faded pajamas as he stretched across old linens on a double bed. I learned later about his reputation as one of the meanest men to come to Norfolk from North Carolina.

Immediately, three things caught my attention. First, the oil stove sitting at the foot of his bed, inches from his old mattress, glowed cherry red. A leaking oil line from the stove wound through the air and poked through the glass window to connect to a barrel outside of the house. Mr. Peoples had removed the stove's carburetor to overheat the already stifling room, which made the sides of the stove bright red and glowing, threatening to explode. The stove itself leaked in several places and black oil soaked the old tar floor covering in his room. Sparks from his wife's wood stove landed precariously near the oil on the floor.

I also noticed roaches. Even in the dark bedroom, I saw them running up and down the walls around me. A door in the back of his room led to a filthy kitchen. The dishes on its shelves appeared alive with roaches. Then, I heard the dog growling. In the back of the kitchen, I saw a big, scraggly street dog standing on some rags that sufficed as his bed. The dog's matted and mangy coat managed to stand up on his neck. He held his head down and showed his teeth as he growled, wanting to attack me.

Under these circumstances, I suggested that we pray. I went back to Mrs. Peoples' bed and stood over her while I prayed for God to heal her. She whispered something during the prayer that I could not understand. Her sister explained to me that Mrs. Peoples had repeated "Thank You, Jesus." I prayed for Mr. Peoples as well. After promising to come back the next day, I went home.

That night, I called Faith Community Church's pastor, Rev. James Drew, and asked him to help me with Mr. Peoples' oil heater. When we entered the home, Mrs. Peoples' miraculous recovery surprised me. The Lord had raised her up from her stroke. Her family gave me the credit for healing her. I helped Pastor Drew repair the heater and clean up the oil-soaked floor covering. We then went out in the backyard with Alford and cut long lumber scraps into firewood, using a powered handsaw. We worked in high grass, full of dog waste. I began to talk with Alford about Jesus when he asked me several times about my reason for helping them.

A few days later, I returned during the evening to talk with Mr. Peoples about his relationship with Jesus Christ. Mr. Peoples shared how he had called three ministers who seemed to ignore him. He felt forsaken by church people and gave up on God. In his dark room, the power of the good news of God's plan for rescuing this needy man suddenly became glorious. Rejoicing in this special moment, I explained to him, from the Bible, how to obtain eternal life, forgiveness, and righteousness from God through faith in Jesus.

Mr. Peoples and I now had a common point of experience, because we had to receive salvation the same way, since all have sinned and fallen short of God's standard of holiness. The same Lord is Lord of all who call on Him.

For everyone who calls on the name of the Lord will be saved.

He responded to the Bible's good news by simply saying, "I never heard it this way." He embraced Jesus as both God and Savior that night and became a new creation. Eventually, he rode his moped to our church and joined our fellowship.

As it turned out, Mr. Peoples had a sincere, kind heart, but few knew it. I cannot begin to tell you about all the blessings that he brought to me. At a time when some made a big deal about my "whiteness," he cherished my visits. He loved my small daughter, Rebekah, and put her picture in the corner of a framed portrait of Jesus, which he proudly hung on his living room wall above his old television set. Every year I brought Rebekah and a group of teenagers to sing Christmas carols at his new apartment, under the scrutiny of the whole neighborhood.

I also witnessed miraculous and intimate times of ministry with him and his family. Mr. Peoples took great pride in keeping the yard mowed at his new apartment. When someone stole his lawnmower, I brought a young person over who boldly asked God to send it back. One year later, it appeared at his apartment, and the Lord greatly strengthened Mr. Peoples' faith.

The Lord also strengthened his wife several times through prayer before she died. We interceded for her unsaved children and Alford. Later, Mr. Peoples surprised the church when drove his moped up to Pastor Drew's yard and handed him $500 for the new church roof. Mr. Peoples never mentioned this gift to anyone.

When Mr. Peoples lay dying of cancer, I visited the public housing apartment where he had moved so that his daughter could take care of him. Entering her apartment, I could hear him moaning in the next room. I looked up and noticed Mr. Peoples' picture of Christ hanging on the wall, with my daughter Rebekah's photo still stuck in the corner of its frame.

When I entered his room, he called me by name. As his sister mopped the floor, she said that I was the only one that he had acknowledged at all. He rocked and moaned in his bed as if he suffered pain that made him delirious. When I prayed for him, I asked God to let him rest. He fell asleep instantly, as peaceful as a baby. Mr. Peoples died a few weeks later, and I preached the gospel to his extended family at the funeral. It rained until the funeral ended. His family members said that the rain proved, as if a sign from God, that Mr. Peoples went to heaven.

The day before the funeral service, I looked at Mr. Peoples' obituary and saw the notice that Missionary Mike Fariss would officiate. Before then, I had never spoken at a funeral. I did not know most of the relatives who filed in after the casket. When it came to my turn to speak, I started by saying that I knew about Mr. Peoples' hard life. The relatives' eyes opened wide with amazement when I went through the Scriptures and Mr. Peoples' testimony, asserting confidently that Mr. Peoples lived in heaven, by the grace of God. His nephew Alford sat in the back of the church, listening intently.

Then all the experiences he had drawn me into were topped off when his family buried him next to an old pig farm. The funeral procession seemed to go on forever. The undertaker led our cars into the country and down a winding, single-lane dirt road to a hidden cemetery. Surrounded by tall pine trees, the cemetery served generations of black families. Pigs grunted in a big mud flat a few yards from the gravesite while I thanked God for letting me know Mr. Peoples and prayed for the family.

Mr. Peoples lived a difficult life. His criminal stepson once said, "I am bad, but not as bad as him. If God can save John Peoples, He can save anybody." Yet the Lord graciously allowed me to serve John Peoples and bring him to Christ.

For the past twenty years, I have grappled with how to exalt Jesus Christ in urban ministry. What model should be used? What methods or programs should be emphasized? God taught me a more important principle through Mr. Peoples, which the Holy Spirit and Scripture confirm. From Mr. Peoples, I learned about my potential for inner-city ministry, which all believers possess, when I clearly proclaimed the gospel message in the power of the Holy Spirit and in the role of a servant. God gave me the blessing of racial reconciliation with Mr. Peoples.

# CHAPTER 4

# Preacher

*Warren Weisner, missionary to New Guinea, speaks at a Faith Baptist Church missions conference. Mike's father, Fred Fariss, sits in background.*

In August 1981, the elders at the Tabernacle Church of Norfolk invited Kim and me to join them around a circle of tables to determine whether they should commission us as full-time inner-city missionaries. This white congregation had opened the Discovery Youth Center in 1976 as an outreach to the public high school, located across the street from the church. They assumed that white students would participate in its after-school program. Instead, black students, bused to school, filled the center while they waited for their extracurricular activities. The Tabernacle Church found itself suddenly thrust into a difficult inner-city ministry. The problems of managing this outreach generated much sentiment in the church toward closing it down. The church also struggled with a financial deficit that happened to be the same amount required by the youth center's budget. I directed this youth center on a part-time basis while I earned a masters of business administration degree from Old Dominion University.

As a couple, Kim and I probably generated more uncertainty for the ministry. Young, and with no formal Bible training at the time, we came along in an era when many leaders around the country argued against white persons becoming involved in ministry in the black community. In addition, I had just graduated from Old Dominion University and needed an increase in salary to accept the job. Fund raising seemed impossible because of my race and our perception that other churches would not respond to our needs. We questioned whether churches would support us to work in another church's ministry.

Veteran missionaries, mother's parents met in Africa and ministered there under the old school philosophy of faith missions. They suffered much hardship through the Depression and war era and were able to return home only once in twenty years. Their second furlough home resulted in tragedy when my grandfather's appendix burst as their ship approached New York City. He died a few days later.

Only four years old, my mother returned to Africa with my grandmother, without her brother and sister. When Mom became ready to enter the seventh grade, Grandma Marsh sent her to a boarding school in the States, while she herself remained in Tanzania. My grandmother retired from the field after forty-five years.

Although he does not talk much about his childhood, I heard that my father, Fred Fariss, grew up in poverty in Portsmouth, Virginia. His father, my grandfather, owned a sign painting business in downtown Norfolk. MacArthur Center Mall now stands on that very location. Dad told me that his father, for some unknown reason, often failed to bring his earnings home after work. This caused financial hardship and marital strife. Since my grandmother purchased groceries on a daily basis back then, she bought food when he brought money home or she fought my grandfather when he did not. My grandfather deserted the family until he returned home to die from lung cancer. The Lord used the war effort to save the family from financial ruin. My dad and his brother dropped out of high school and became apprentices at the Norfolk Naval Shipyard in Portsmouth, where my grandmother also found work. The Army drafted my father and he served a year in Korea. When he returned to Portsmouth, he participated in Youth for Christ ministries, which led to his enrollment in a southern Bible college, thanks to the GI Bill. Dad met Mom at this Bible college.

This occurred between 1950 and 1954 in the turbulent years preceding the forced integration of colleges in the South. Dad rejected his college's segregation enrollment policies during his freshman year. After an unsuccessful appeal for black enrollment, Dad regularly attended Sunday services with black congregations. He also taught Bible classes and discipled black young people, traveling up to fifty miles to meet with them. After my parents married, my dad taught for a year at a Bible institute in Tennessee, which white college administrators established to equip black church leaders. My parents served there with no financial support except the food that a white Presbyterian church collected for them. I became aware of this family history years after I started serving in the inner city. A black church leader, whom Dad had assisted, told me of my father's early ministry with African-Americans. I had always wondered why some black leaders highly respected him.

As a child, I knew that we gave up a lot, but I did not want it any other way. My parents moved to Portsmouth and then to Virginia Beach where they established a Baptist church. They continued to make financial sacrifices for the ministry. Every day I gave up my dad who worked seven days a week. Every four years, I gave my grandmother back to the Africans. Over and over I provided my bed for visiting missionaries. When my father made a faith promise challenge at church, I did not hesitate to pledge my grass-cutting money and more.

The host of missionary speakers, camps, conferences, and hours my dad spent discussing world missions with visiting missionaries were not lost on me. At age seven, I sensed my need for God's salvation. Before a Sunday evening service, I talked to my father about it. He explained John 3:16, introduced me to Christ, and asked me to give my testimony in front of the church.

At nine years old, I also made a serious decision to become a full-time missionary to New Guinea. I corresponded with Warren and Mary Weisner, who served there for many years. Norfolk Christian Schools, where I attended elementary school, sponsored annual missions conferences that challenged me. Our church also conducted a missions conference every year. At one conference, I noticed the banner posted on the wall next to where I sat in the church that quoted William Carey: "Expect great things from God; attempt great things for God." At that moment, I made a covenant with God, asking for an assignment that others were unwilling or unable to fulfill.

As I turned thirteen, the church embarked on the Coral Ridge Evangelism Explosion program. While in a class for teens, I learned over thirty salvation scriptures, wrote and presented my testimony, and began using its outline to explain the gospel. This course grounded my faith in a gospel that I could clearly understand and explain to others.

In the next two years, the Lord blessed me with opportunities to witness for Christ aggressively from bed to bed at the Public Health Hospital, at a nursing home, at camps, through door-to-door visitation, after Good News Child Evangelism Fellowship clubs, at the Union (Rescue) Mission, and to my friends at Princess Anne High School in suburban Virginia Beach. In the ninth grade, this effort earned me the title of "preacher" at school. I led a friend to Christ in the stadium bleachers during PE class. I remember preaching the gospel during my science class report on "Why I Do Not Believe in Evolution."

Before community league basketball games, our coach asked me to lead the team prayer. I always ended with a request that everyone on the team would understand why Jesus died for us on the cross. Committed to evangelism that year, I told the varsity high school basketball coach that I would not try out for the junior varsity team. I explained about my commitment to Jesus Christ and my involvement in ministry.

I also learned that if I took time to meditate on scripture in preparation for a sermon or lesson, God would speak and give me an exhortation. The Lord gave me several opportunities to preach or teach in those years.

As a high school freshman, on my youth leader's advice meant for the young adults in our church, I began praying for God to send me a wife. In tenth grade, I had the very special privilege of leading Kim to Christ on her front porch. We dated six years before we married.

In tenth grade, I also made the junior varsity basketball team, and God gave me an outstanding season. Unfortunately, this success revealed a lot about my motives for evangelism. In retrospect, I spent much of the previous "spiritual" year seeking my dad's and my peers' acceptance. Then I substituted the prestige of high school athletics for the church youth group. I demoted Jesus Christ and my vows to serve Him below my basketball goals and dreams.

By the grace of God, He intervened in my junior year with a devastating knee injury, which broke me. In a way that only the Lord can do, I experienced years of frustration, humiliation, and loss that lasted until after I turned twenty-two. I regret deeply that I failed to live for Christ while I enjoyed so much influence through basketball.

# CHAPTER 5

# Black!

*Mike at Princess Anne High School 1974*

In all these experiences, God hid a work in my life that I did not notice until years later in urban ministry. On our long school bus rides to and from Norfolk Christian Lower School, we passed several black communities. I thought a lot about the ways they differed from my own neighborhood. I often asked myself, "Why are their houses different? Why do they have asphalt siding? Why are these people poor?" But the thought that stirred me the most, even at a young age, concerned questions about what African-Americans must think, what they must feel. In other words, I wanted to understand the black experience.

This awareness grew through my father's ministry. In his own pastoral work, he continued to confront segregation and remained involved in training and consulting black church leaders. One such pastor, Rev. James Earls, joined our church and served as a missionary with Child Evangelism Fellowship (CEF). He spent several years ministering and studying with my dad while he prepared for ordination and, eventually, church-planting work. During this time that my father mentored him, Rev. Earls took other teenagers and me into the old slums that used to exist in Hampton Roads. There we conducted five-day Bible clubs in his CEF "Chapel on Wheels." My awareness of the black community grew as I spent many hours in ministry with him and his family.

On one occasion, for example, Rev. Earls brought some of us into a public housing community center. I wandered into an auditorium where black teenage girls rehearsed on a small stage. Wooden chairs, left disorganized in front of the stage, gave me a good place to watch them as I sat alone. The girls wore shorts and T-shirts and had large Afro hairstyles. I remember that their attitudes seemed defiant. In their late teens, their performance fascinated me. They sang loudly and danced in unison, and as I watched, their music seemed to build up to loud stomping and singing. The girls finished with a hard stomp and the proud shout of one word, "Black!" On this word, they simultaneously dropped their heads and shoved their fists into the air. Every girl froze in this militant pose. A hush fell on the auditorium at this ending.

After the program, I quietly walked outside to the street where Rev. Earls held a Good News Club in his portable Chapel on Wheels. Child Evangelism Fellowship provided a trailer that the pastor pulled behind his old car and that looked like a miniature church. When we drove into a slum area or public housing community, the pastor would ring a bell, just like an ice cream truck. Children poured out of the open hallways of deteriorated apartment buildings to meet in our clubs.

During this ministry with Rev. Earls, I realized that I participated in rare experiences for a white person. I did not think much of it then, but I remember how much I loved being in the inner-city neighborhoods, in spite of the perceived danger. On one occasion, as we stood around relaxing after our ministry, I thought about how good I felt working there. I noticed a special joy. Even though my mind told me that I did not belong, my heart burdened me to stay.

God began to give me personal successes in cross-racial ministry, which boosted my faith. After giving invitations during these Bible clubs, Pastor Earls often asked me to counsel children who responded to the invitation, and I led them to Christ. He also spoke at our church's summer camp. With other young people and committed adult volunteers, my family joined in with his camp ministry and served many young people from low-income backgrounds.

My dad and Mr. Earls used their relationship to promote racial reconciliation through the gospel. Several upperclassmen in our youth group successfully asked their history teachers to invite these men to public school history classes to discuss white and black church relations. At summer camps, I witnessed the respect and love that the men showed each other. They both loved, and worked hard with, difficult teenagers, and I watched them sit down and personally share the gospel with many of them. I remember praying, "Lord, give me a double portion of these men's spirits." I wanted to minister like them.

During our special discipleship camp program, Rev. Earls dropped me with other teenagers along the road in rural North Carolina to witness for Christ in an African-American community. I remember knocking on a screen door, holding up a gospel tract to two black teenage girls, and asking, "Do you know where you will be five minutes after you die?" They said no, and I asked if I could share from the Bible the way to know for sure. They invited us into their living room. We sat down and I read the tract to them. Both girls made decisions for Christ. Letters I received from one of them confirmed their commitments.

Playing high school basketball gave opportunities to establish friendships with black athletes. My white friend, Ray Ellis, started a fad among white players on the team when he dressed and talked like a black movie hero named "Superfly." I somehow began relating to the black teammates "for real." I felt respected by them. Before the start of a basketball game, my sophomore season, a black teammate shook my hand at the center jump. Because we won the game we continued the ritual before every contest. It became a way to communicate our friendship and to get us psyched up. Years later, I realized that he had taught me to "slap." Without trying, I broke the ice with black young people and men, just by using that grasp that communicated mutual respect.

I also developed close friendships in college with three black students at different times. One accepted Christ several years later at the Discovery Center. I also worked my way through college at a kitchen with Betty, a black woman in her mid-thirties. Our friendship provided my first opportunity to learn how to communicate respect and openness with the female side of the culture.

After Kim and I married, this background gave me the confidence to volunteer with Rev. Vernon Watford at the Triple C Bible Camp in North Carolina, which served black young people in rural North Carolina. All these experiences came to a head there. I asked for the Lord's forgiveness and asked to be re-commissioned. I remembered my childhood commitment, certain that God would make me take Kim to New Guinea. But my will broke, and I received a deep conviction that I would go anywhere and do anything for Christ.

I also remember asking the Lord again to send me somewhere that others did not want to go or believed they could not go. In addition, I asked the Lord, by His grace, to allow me to introduce people to Himself as my assignment. Though hard to explain, zeal for the Lord broke open in me there. Kim spent thirty minutes with me when I returned home and declared that she did not know me. The Lord radically changed me that summer. But God had not finished preparing me.

Until then, I had never heard of a white person ministering full-time in the black community. No one in Norfolk ever considered this as an option for us. As a result, we applied with a mission board to go to Haiti, and two significant things happened. First, my missionary commitment prompted me to take an international management class. Although in a secular class, I discovered prejudices in my thinking related to my ethnocentric perspective of the world. I began working through preconceived racial values most consistent with normal, white Christian sentiments but rooted in feelings of superiority. I dealt with several hang-ups as God prepared me for cross-cultural ministry.

Then, the mission board requested that I receive ministry experience while I attended graduate school. With my experience at Triple C Bible Camp, I volunteered at Tabernacle Church of Norfolk's Discovery Youth Center. There it hit me. In this after-school program, zeal for ministry in the black community took hold of me. The burden came from deep within my soul. Unshakable conviction that God called me to this kind of ministry gripped me. I remember helping Rich Hardison, the associate pastor of the Tabernacle Church of Norfolk at the time, work on his porch roof. As we talked about my application for Haiti, Rich asked , "Mike, what has God burdened you to do?" I responded immediately, "Minister in the black community." We stared at each other, contemplating the ramifications of what I had just said. I had found my assignment from God.

CHAPTER 6

# Stop Trying— You'll Never Be Black

*Discovery Youth Center recreation room 1981*

The Lord tested my sense of calling right away through the discouraging responses of other Christians. When I began directing the Discovery Youth Center, I received negative feedback from all directions. Pastor Garrick, the senior pastor, seemed disappointed because I had changed my plans about Haiti. He also tactfully said that he was not totally convinced that a white person could work in the inner city. The only one in my family who encouraged me was my retired missionary grandmother, Margaret Marsh, who lived in Florida. Fortunately, God gave Kim the faith, through her mother's encouragement, to support me in my seemingly crazy ideas, or we would not have made it together.

A black leader chided me by accusing me of trying to be the great white hope. Another black pastor complained that I taught white doctrine. That summer I took a busload of teens to a ministry for black young people. When I stepped off the bus to greet the ministry's director, his first words were a hurtful rebuke: "Stop trying to be black. You'll never be black, so stop trying."

To make matters worse, during my first year in ministry, Jim Jones manipulated and massacred black people in Guyana. Several blacks who opposed my involvement easily compared me to the cult leader. Raising support from white churches added to my frustration. Not long after I began, I met with a missions committee chairman to seek financial support from his large, white, evangelical church. We sat across the table at breakfast. After I tried to explain my work with young people, he asked about my children. Then he said, "You can say what you want about ministry, but I can assure you that no spear-chuckers will come anywhere near my daughters." Then the next pastor I visited told me that he could not consider supporting me because they had already done something related to black people that year. He said that his elders would not allow any more black issues for a while. He also said that they had started a program for black children but stopped when some members complained about the smell.

I also heard white Christians question the legitimacy of my ministry because of my race, because they wanted Christians to remain segregated, because they resented the way Norfolk neighborhoods deteriorated after they moved out, or because the need for overseas missionaries remained so great. My father's church, where I grew up and learned evangelism, dropped our support after he left because we did not serve in a Baptist ministry.

Things also grew difficult in the ministry. The administration and coaches at the high school across the street from the Discovery Youth Center refused to cooperate with us. At first, the students acted violently and abused the youth center's facility, negatively impacting the church's other ministries. Many students smoked marijuana outside the center. When it turned real cold, they stepped inside the door, and the smell of pot or cigarettes rose through the building. Before shootings became common, the guys and girls engaged in frequent fistfights. They carried knives, belts, locks, and box cutters to the school and into our facility.

My sense of calling and my love for ministry took me through this tough beginning. I confess that I also started with an attitude. I often said to myself, "My grandfather died ministering to black people in Africa. No one complained about him giving his life overseas; I will let no one discourage me." I wrote Grandma Marsh a letter describing my intentions to remain in the States and not serve as a foreign missionary. The letter probably sounded like an apology for not going to Africa. She wrote me a beautiful response, telling me how she had helped conduct Bible clubs in low-income neighborhoods near her retirement village in Florida. She wrote about her burden to pray for needy families there. My grandmother's endorsement powerfully encouraged me.

Soon Pastor Gene Garrick of the Tabernacle Church of Norfolk invited Dr. John Perkins to come to his office and consult us on what to do at the Discovery Youth Center. I sat silently in the midst of two highly respected Christian leaders. Dr. Perkins had successfully founded several Christian community development outreaches, including Voice of Calvary Ministries. Pastor Garrick had established Norfolk Christian Schools, and then, while senior pastor, became an international leader in the Christian school movement and world missions.

Between several meetings, the Lord provided a quiet moment when Pastor Garrick and I sat alone with Dr. Perkins. I remained quiet while Pastor Garrick relayed my vision for ministry in the inner city. Dr Perkins began speaking very slowly. Although he talked in such a way that it seemed like he was speaking to Pastor Garrick, he leaned forward and looked directly into my eyes. I had no doubt that he wanted me to take his words personally. He said something like this: "We have a lot of people who talk about helping the poor, but we do not have many with commitment. We need people with commitment." As he looked hard at me, I felt like Peter when Jesus said that he would deny Him thrice.

I dared not respond. I was twenty-three years old. I dared not say to this man who had endured so much suffering during the Civil Rights movement that I had commitment. But inside I said it. I remember saying to myself, "Mr. Perkins, time will prove to you that I have the commitment it takes." Still, his challenge encouraged me. He had not mentioned my race. He had only said that I needed commitment, and I surely had enough of that. After Dr. Perkin's visit, Lem Tucker, President of Voice of Calvary Ministries until his death, came to Norfolk and conducted a week-long seminar on the VOC model. Dr. Perkins eventually published this model in his book, *Justice for All.*

My belief in the power of God and in God's love for families living in Norfolk's low-income neighborhoods blessed me as well. I held the conviction that the ministry belonged to the Lord; it was up to Him to make it successful. When I first opened the youth center, fifty black young people came up to enjoy the card game "spades" or the activities we offered in our game room. Alone in the ministry when the school year began, I did not know how I would reach them.

One day they came upstairs to the youth center to find the game room locked off for a Bible study. Many stampeded out of the building at the prospect of the Bible discussion. I remember the tension as I walked out of my office and faced thirty teenagers who sat silently, staring unhappily at me. I asked them for a chance to become their friend and walked back into my office.

In the past, I broke through this type of situation by playing basketball. Now I prayed, "Lord, I cannot play basketball in here. Please make a way. Send me a 'Barnabas' to break the ice." With that, in walked Nathaniel Obey, looking for a part-time job while he attended college.

Nat and I knew each other from Old Dominion University. I had met him when I went to the gym with my chemistry lab partner for a few pick-up basketball games. He pointed out Nat as one of the best players in intramural basketball. I had a lot of frustration with basketball still pent up inside because I had never achieved my goals. When our turn came up to play, I went after Nat right away. We still debate who won out that day, but we ended up as friends.

The summer before I became the Discovery Youth Center Director, I opened the Norfolk Christian High School gym on Saturday nights for public high school players. Nat coached a high school basketball summer league team and heard that a white man had opened a gym. He walked in with about fifteen players. As they warmed up, I mentioned to him that we usually began with a devotional time. Nat immediately turned and ordered the team to sit down. I found myself standing before some big guys. One turned out to be Bruce Smith, later of the Buffalo Bills and Washington Redskins.

After the Lord gave us an awesome devotion and tough basketball games, Nat rested with Kim and me outside the gym. Referring to the devotion, Nat claimed to be a Christian because of his church membership and baptism. I mentioned my need for help at the center in the coming fall semester, but he turned me down. He boasted about having a good paying job waiting for him when he returned to ODU in the fall. Two months later, Nat visited me when his job had mysteriously fallen through. Within weeks he accepted Christ and began aggressively witnessing for Him at the Discovery Center. We worked together for two years before he moved to Washington, DC, where he serves as a pastor.

Although high school students behaved violently back then, God blessed us to establish bonds with some of the fiercest fighters in the school. Among the boys, the toughest two were Hotdog, the captain of the football team, and Bugeye, someone whom everyone said lived in the worst part of the city. Three girls also became friends with Nat and me. They often fought like boys and intimidated the rest of the girls at school. Once, when a boy pulled a knife on Hotdog in the gym, he took off his belt, wrapped it around his fist and began fighting back. After the teachers pulled Hotdog away, his sister stepped up and continued punching the boy with the knife like a boxer going for the knockout.

These young people came to the Discovery Center and headed straight for my office to talk with me. One day, two of the girls asked if abortion was murder. I took them through the Bible to show that God creates a person at conception, not at birth. Two weeks after one had her baby, I sat in the stands at a high school boy's basketball game waiting for the overtime period to begin. Suddenly, the girl who just had the baby and another one of the girls ran out of the stands. In a wild flurry of punches, they began beating up a girl from the other school before a capacity crowd, in the center of the basketball court. About nine years later, the baby born to my young friend became the star quarterback on the city's dominating recreation football team. I coached teams that endured humiliating losses to his team. These games did not bother me as much because I rejoiced that God let me help save the quarterback's unborn life. During the time that he played on this community team, his mother died in a tragic car accident.

To my knowledge, none of these young people made commitments to Christ. They attended all the Bible studies and made them quite lively. But our close friendships with these tough leaders communicated something about me to the rest of the student body. The acceptance among black students that I won through them resonated throughout their neighborhoods.

Although we made a lot of mistakes those first years, I never felt a racial barrier with unsaved young people. My relationship with Nat settled the issue almost immediately. Soon, two black coaches made commitments to Christ and provided opportunities for me to work in partnership with the high school.

CHAPTER 7

# Willing
# Obedience

I lost count of the number of men who expressed a calling to this type of outreach but said that they refused to respond because of their wives' opposition or fears. During our twenty years of ministry, many people asked about my wife, Kim, and her ability to cope with inner-city ministry. Kim's journey through this experience was not easy, to say the least. Yet, her faithfulness blessed me immeasurably. Her testimony benefits other wives facing this urban calling.

Before meeting Kim in our tenth-grade geometry class, I heeded our youth pastor's advice and started praying that God would show me my wife. At age fourteen, in the early seventies, I attended a public high school during the miniskirt, "hot pants," and bra-less look. I figured it was time to settle down. When I walked into geometry class and noticed Kim, I somehow knew that God had just introduced me to my future wife.

I enjoyed the privilege of leading Kim to Christ on a New Year's Eve. Immediately, as young teenagers, we began planning our timetable for marriage. Unfortunately, no one followed up her decision for Christ. We became each other's source of strength and temptation at the same time. As a result, she missed a foundation of discipleship needed to put us on the same spiritual footing in our marriage.

Kim also became one of the most popular girls in high school. By the time we graduated, she had won about everything possible. When we argued, most of the student body, our class sponsor, my family, and even my black teammates took her side and confronted me. Many students regarded her as the most socially powerful girl in our class of over 700 students. We dated six years and wed in her home church, without thinking about ministry. She started her career as an office manager, and I pursued a master's degree in business. As high school sweethearts, Kim and I failed to prepare for both marriage and ministry.

Kim's process of adapting to urban outreach began abruptly when I returned from Triple C Bible Camp. With my calling renewed, our preparations to become foreign missionaries tested her commitment to Christ for the first time. Fortunately, she demonstrated the grace of God by setting a policy of following my headship because of her sincere fear of the Lord and her mother's advice. Although she felt some concerns about my career, from the beginning, my late mother-in-law, Joanne Cervell, strongly encouraged Kim to support me in my work.

When we started ministering at the Discovery Center, every small step of faith I took amounted to a giant leap for her. Often alone in ministry, Kim did not have a support system and endured the negative consequences of my efforts. I worked full time while getting my MBA and took no days off. Young people and interns often stayed at our house, while needy people pulled me away for various reasons and at all hours. The negative way many people treated me in the beginning also disturbed her. All these factors forced her to work through resentment against my vision for outreach.

To make this process more challenging, Kim went through culture shock. Raised in a small Presbyterian church that always started on time and ended promptly at twelve noon, Kim had to adjust to a different time culture. She learned to cope with a schedule that many times frustrated her organized, detail-oriented, and time-conscious nature.

The Lord also helped Kim confront her racist attitudes. I remember taking her to an inner-city recreation function that turned out to be too long, disorganized, and boring. When we finally left, and as we approached our pickup truck, she chided me for parking in a pile of glass. She became enraged when she realized that the glass came from our truck's window. Mistaking my Bible cover for a pocketbook, someone broke into my truck and stole my study Bible! Kim rode home in a seat full of broken glass, yelling all the while a host of racist expletives. When she looked to me for agreement, I said that the truck belonged to the Lord, and if He let someone break His window, then it was His problem. Kim accused me of drifting off into a spiritual cloud. The experience with the truck window highlighted her fear that I was going to get myself killed. As I made myself vulnerable, she fought her own insecurity.

I share all this to make the point that God took Kim through a difficult growth process to help her understand our potential for urban cross-racial ministry. She learned to minister willingly through obedience.

CHAPTER 8

# Who Is That White Guy?

*Mike in an evangelistic Halloween program 1985*

This process included the decision facing the Tabernacle Church elders in August 1981 regarding our future in their Discovery Youth Center ministry. That evening, the Lord spoke again. When it came time for me to address them, I simply said that I planned to minister in Norfolk's black community regardless of the future of the Discovery Center and put the decision into their hands. Kim said she would do anything I wanted, and then we went home.

I am not sure what happened after we left. Somehow God established in their hearts the conviction that He wanted them to expand the church's inner-city ministry, even in the face of their deficit, to commission us as full-time missionaries, to begin our deputation, and to send us to work through Faith Community Church in an impoverished neighborhood.

From then until his death, Pastor Garrick championed our ministry, believing that God had made His will known in these decisions. Interestingly, the Lord provided our extra support within days, and within months, supplied the funds to meet the deficit in the missions budget. Tabernacle Church committed to this missions venture and commissioned Kim and me as full-time urban missionaries. Royster Memorial Presbyterian Church and several families also joined our partnership team and faithfully provided financial and prayer support for twenty years.

Before long, I met Ken Watson in Huntersville, where he worked as a juvenile probation officer. Interested in partnering with the Fellowship of Christian Athletes, we volunteered as "huddle" sponsors in two different public high schools. We became close friends through our hard work with young people. We learned how to compliment each other's gifts and talents. The FCA gave us opportunities to take busloads of high school athletes to breakfasts, weekend retreats, and summer camps.

God blessed our FCA outreach when Ken's former high school football coach asked him to conduct chapel services before their football games. At the start of the season, a car accident killed the star running back, and Ken comforted the player's family, the coaches, and the team. His chapel times before the games inspired them to upset their opponents, and they advanced to the state championship.

His success opened the door for me to become the chaplain for another high school football team in our city. This school had failed to win a game in three previous years. Our pre-game chapel services at both schools created opportunities to build strong relationships with coaches and players. Ken and I helped these teams and a lot of young people succeed through these avenues.

The week before our two teams played each other, the other leaders at our church joked that the game would prove who was more spiritual, Ken or I. They teased that winning the game would show whose prayers possessed more power with God since we conducted chapel services at the same time in different locker rooms. Ken and I boldly asserted that God would let the game finish in a tie to solve the dilemma, since back then, high schools did not break tied football games in overtime periods.

The teams played at Foreman Field, a large stadium in Norfolk. Ken and I arrived with our respective teams. As I walked out on the Astroturf under the bright lights, I could see Ken on the other side of the field. The teams began their warm-up exercises, and I felt intense emotion in their warm-ups. The winner would possess first place in the district race.

Ken and I walked toward each other at the same time. We met on the fifty-yard line in the middle of the football field. On some kind of spiritual impulse, we bowed our heads and prayed together. Our prayers had nothing to do h winning the game. We prayed for God to use our ministries in the locker room to touch the hearts of the players and coaches. We asked God for the chance to bring glory to Jesus Christ through our high school outreach. We prayed for all the coaches and players on the field.

The game took a dramatic course that encouraged our commitment to this sports ministry. After the warm-up drills, I followed the players as they ran back to the locker room for my chapel service. The coaches settled them down, gave a few last minute instructions, and left the team with me. Usually, the team would bust out of the locker room and jump out to an early lead. This game started differently. Almost immediately after I began to challenge the team, the assistant coaches threw open the steel doors and called the team out. The players ran out of the locker room without a devotion or prayer. I could picture in my mind Ken fervently praying in the other locker room. His team wasted no time putting his devotion into practice. They quickly took the early lead and held the game's momentum. Then the Lord turned the game on its head as the other team ran a play toward our side of the field.

Five players on Ken's team pulled out in front of their running back, creating a surge intended to run down our team's defensive end and backs. Instead, they overran them and smashed into the sidelines. The heart of their "sweep" hit our team's head football coach and broke both of his legs. The game's first half ended, and our coaches sent the team to locker room while they arranged for the head coach to go to the emergency room. I followed the team under the bleachers, the only adult who entered the locker room with them. I found the players, badly beaten in the first half, divided against each other. Most of the black players made angry comments about their white teammates, accusing them of playing scared. The white players looked scared to me.

I made a suggestion. I said, "Why don't we pray since we didn't get a chance before the game. Let's do it right." Most of the players knelt immediately. Two of the black players needed coaxing by the others, but they also kneeled. After we prayed, they returned to the field and turned the game around. They play most inspired this half of the game, still without their head coach. In the last minutes of the game, our team tied the score. The opposing coach downed the football to end the game, even with enough time remaining for one more play, because our team threatened to come back with such high intensity. As we predicted, the game ended with a tie score. More importantly, our work with coaches and players in Norfolk took off. As a result, Ken became FCA's full time area director for Hampton Roads, and I served on his board.

Working with Ken in FCA gave me great confidence. Ken demonstrated impressive speaking ability. Big build, black, intimidating, funny, and gracious, he became a great crossover speaker. His animated style won over blacks and whites, young and old. As an evangelist in the pulpit, Ken saw God bless his many salvation messages with results. Ken also ministered as a gifted teacher and wise leader.

Because of these qualities, people recruited Ken to speak. When he took these opportunities, impressed people often made him job offers. People usually assumed that he had all the spiritual gifts because he could preach well. Interest in hearing from a white guy who ministered in inner-city ministry remained low, so Ken's voice spoke for both of us.

Ken and I complemented each other's gifts and ministry priorities. I contributed to Ken my fearless commitment to minister to the poor. I also functioned as the visionary and plan-maker. I emphasized personal evangelism. Ken's gift of evangelism became evident in the pulpit; mine in one-to-one witnessing. During his work with FCA, I served as Ken's sounding board. He discussed strategy and procedures. He used them dynamically and impacted FCA ministries around the country.

When Ken's black associates saw me hanging around him during FCA retreats, they usually asked: "Who is that white guy?" I know Ken amazed some of them with his commitment to me. I also know that he caught some grief from a few of his black associates for sticking with me so tightly; but we partnered in true fellowship.

"Iron sharpened iron" for five years, as we grew closer. Ken and I took college-credited Bible classes together at the Norfolk Bible Institute, an extension of Washington Bible College. We studied in small classrooms in a large, stately house that Faith Community Church renovated during this time. We froze in the winter; perspired in the summer. The gas heater's blower tried to drown out the teachers. During the summer, the windows, with no screens, stayed open. The noise from the nearby street life gave the classes a distinctive urban flavor.

Dr. Ken Brackney taught us Bible in this extension school. Ken Watson and I studied, analyzed, debated, tested, and implemented Dr. Brackney's personal instruction in our day-to-day ministries. For his part, Dr. Brackney elevated the scope and difficulty of our Bible classes to be comparable to seminary course work. We carried everything we learned to the Discovery Center, to FCA retreats, or to our church ministries where we fleshed them out. Our growth occurred under the oversight of Pastors Garrick and Hardison at the Tabernacle Church and Pastor Drew at Faith Community Church.

During this special time of collaboration, Ken and I sensed God's leading to establish our vision for ministry together. We dedicated ourselves to become church planters and target impoverished families for several critical reasons. First, church planting reached adults, especially men. We observed many needs related to family problems passed down from parents to children, ensnaring persons in poverty. Church planting evangelism gave us the potential to target men and equip them for leadership to break poverty cycles.

Second, Ken and I appreciated church planting's flexibility to quickly organize churches with new approaches to family intervention, accountability, and comprehensive discipleship. We wanted to structure churches to intervene with family substance abuse, immorality, illiteracy, school dropout, teen pregnancy, and unemployment.

Third, church planting motivated us to empower new indigenous spiritual leaders within inner-city communities. Ken and I determined to equip them to evangelize and minister in their own neighborhoods. This included elevating these leaders to full participation in the Great Commission at home and abroad and providing them with formal Bible training. Church planting created opportunities and a demand for indigenous leaders who proved effective in community evangelism. We envisioned incorporating formal Bible training into the Christian education ministries of the new churches.

Fourth, church planting presented opportunities to reach diverse populations of residents without the hindrances of segregated worship. We saw the benefit of mobilizing church planting teams to use their cultural, racial, and socioeconomic diversity as an advantage when reaching unchurched persons from low-income backgrounds.

Last, we intended to plant churches structured to evangelize at-risk young people. We wanted to make parent evangelism a priority, along with addressing family education and substance abuse problems. This included the desire to elevate church leaders who relate well to the urban youth culture.

Our vision for church planting became a bond between us. Ken continued to turn down ministry and employment offers to keep himself aligned with our vision. To prepare for this future opportunity, he moved to South Carolina for three years and earned the Master Divinity degree from Columbia Biblical Seminary at Columbia International University. A number of people told me that I made a mistake by encouraging Ken's departure to seminary. Yet I found that the more Ken grew in his own potential, the more his commitment grew to our vision for church planting. The farther we traveled apart, the more we thought like-minded about our future objectives. We empowered each other from a distance. When Ken spoke around the country, people invariable asked him, "What do you do?" Ken shared our vision for church planting, which opened doors for UDM and me. Actually, I could only be happy about Ken leaving town to go to seminary in the South. I felt that God had let me help advance my dad's cause of racial reconciliation in Bible training there.

After Ken left, the scope of our work became broader than the Tabernacle Church of Norfolk. For this reason, we incorporated and adopted the name, Urban Discovery Ministries. Under Tim Seviour's leadership as board president, we embraced a vision for mobilizing urban missionaries and church volunteers.

CHAPTER 9

# Why Won't God Help Me?

About the same time that crack cocaine sales escalated in Huntersville, the Tabernacle Church of Norfolk brought together the leaders of its four extension ministries: Norfolk Christian Schools, the Triple-R Ranch, the National Institute for Learning Disabilities, and Urban Discovery Ministries. In God's awesome timing, these ministries hired a consultant for strategic planning when we needed to redefine our purpose during this drug crisis.

UDM established its mission statement and identified "critical success factors, the elements of ministry deemed vital to the organization's success." Our foremost success factor, upon which we founded our ministry, underscored our commitment to build youth outreach upon a comprehensive ministry that evangelized whole families. I learned the hard way that youth ministries must intervene with young people's parents in the homes to succeed in the inner city.

I discovered this factor in my first year of ministry when I tried to mentor a nine-year-old named Corey. He made a commitment to Christ at a Bible school picnic. After his decision, we participated in so many activities together that I cannot list them all. When I helped him with his homework, I noticed that he was extremely bright and discerning. But Corey quit when problems grew difficult. In other areas besides academics, he showed a tendency to give up and act incorrigible whenever he faced frustrations. Cory lived in a small apartment in a neighborhood that the city soon condemned and tore down. He told me about hearing gunshots in the walled graveyard behind his apartment. During this time, a robber stripped a man and chained him naked to a fence on Corey's street. In spite of all this, Corey showed unusually mature spiritual insight and sensitivity during our Bible clubs.

One day as we drove through his inner-city neighborhood, he stumped me with three questions. He asked, "Does God answer us when we pray?" I replied too quickly, "Sure. If we pray according to His will." Tears began to roll down Corey's cheeks as he responded, "Don't you think God wants my dad to stop drinking and go to work? I pray for this every night and nothing happens. Why won't God help me?" Corey's questions caught me off guard. At that time I lacked solutions for his father's problem. I said, "Don't give up; keep praying, Corey." But Corey did give up—on God and on a lot more.

Corey started to drop out of our activities, so I went to see him and his parents. When I asked his dad about his unemployment, he gave me excuses why he quit several jobs. Inside, I struggled with how to respond. More than anything, I wanted to tell this man that his alcoholism and irresponsibility hurt his son. I wanted to bring up Corey's tendency to quit when faced with difficult problems. I knew that God was pinpointing the spiritual stronghold in the home. But I said nothing because I felt afraid of his parents and their environment.

Corey's parents intimidated me. They were raising three teenagers and I had none. I was twenty-four years old, scared of them, and afraid of everything on their street. I rationalized my behavior by saying the parents seemed hopeless, forcing me to disciple Corey without confronting his father. Besides, I rationalized, some inner-city ministries promoted the idea that we should raise up a new generation of leadership by focusing our ministries on young people, instead of their parents. Unfortunately, my plan did not work out that way. Corey dropped out of school, abused alcohol, and became a leader in the same drug conspiracy that recruited Tito. Eventually, the federal court incarcerated him, and he converted to Islam.

With the coming of crack and its impact on Tito and Chris, God graciously gave me the determination to confront other parents and challenge them to repent and place their faith in Jesus Christ. The crisis threatening to destroy these young people motivated me to take action. With Gina Miller's help, I visited parents and directly called them to repentance and faith in Jesus Christ.

I became determined to boldly challenge Brenda, Tito's mother, with the gospel. While out visiting parents, Gina and I found her. Her quiet presence in her home answered our prayers that she not slip out the back door when we arrived. After five years of resisting our witness, God used the fatal overdose of the man who lived with her and the threat of the streets to her sons to convince Brenda that she needed a Savior. He prepared her heart for the challenge that I gave her to repent from her destructive behavior.

As I shared God's plan of salvation with Brenda, I noticed on her coffee table a ceramic centerpiece. It depicted a lamb next to an open Bible. The painted words on the white ceramic Bible declared: "Behold the Lamb of God." I used the centerpiece to explain how Jesus Christ was the

Lamb who died as God's perfect sacrifice for our sin. By God's grace, Brenda believed in Jesus Christ. Brenda confessed her marijuana smoking habit. She wept as she expressed her faith in Christ in a prayer.

The Lord established our Bible institute and cell church in Brenda's living room. She showed her love and appreciation to Jesus by quietly sobbing in deep gratitude when we celebrated the Lord's table in her home. Each time my mind would picture the forgiven woman who knelt and wiped Christ's feet with her tears. This scene came alive in the Village with Brenda.

Brenda's addiction and the environment in the Village hindered her discipleship. When she relapsed into drug use, she would disappear and avoid us again. Other new converts also struggled. Gina and I visited parents in the Village almost every Sunday afternoon. I mentored a foster teen, Felton Woodson, and took him with me on many home visits I made there. Other times I went alone. During the next twelve months, five more adults made decisions for Christ.

# CHAPTER 10

# Pains of Childbirth

During my first ten years of urban ministry, I used camping and athletic programs to reach kids. In 1990, we took the next step and used these programs to create opportunities to evangelize their parents. With this new priority, we witnessed to many parents, trusting God for the results. Many persons chose to continue their addiction to drugs rather than to surrender to Jesus. Most of them "bottomed out" and lost everything, including their children.

I continued to intercede with God through prayer for the parents' salvation. God faithfully allowed me to see His power to intervene in severe situations. I remember visiting a mother who informed me that she intended to commit sui..e on that particular day. She said that she planned to get a gun and kill herself. She refused any suggestions that I made for her to get help. After I left, I went straight to a nearby phone booth and called the city's crisis hot line. A counselor agreed to meet me at the woman's house. The mother had left before we arrived, and I became concerned that she was looking for a gun.

I stood in her parking lot with the counselor. We both felt helpless and frustrated. As we waited, I stepped aside several times to cry out to God. I said over and over to the Lord, "Where is Your power?" After waiting almost an hour, the woman walked into the parking lot. When she saw me with the counselor, she took off running toward her apartment. Suddenly, and out of nowhere, four police cars full of officers came screeching up to us. Out they jumped with guns drawn and surrounded the area like a SWAT team! They ran past us and took the woman into custody and then to the hospital. Afterward, they asked the counselor for the name of the minister who had called them to report an attempted suicide and a gun. The police assumed that I was the pastor who called 911. The counselor informed them that I could not have called the police because I stood with him in the parking lot for at least an hour. Not finding this minister upset the police. Although we never discovered who placed the 911 call, I left the incident knowing that God could powerfully intervene, even by bringing the police.

In another instance, I walked through the crack cocaine court of the Village to seek out the mother of a child on my flag football team. My walk took me past drug dealers who gambled with their profits. When I arrived, the mother and her boyfriend had just finished smoking crack but invited me into their apartment anyway. I sat down with the boyfriend, but the mother left the apartment. I asked if I could pray. As I prayed, it seemed that time stopped for a moment, as if the Lord and I called a time out. Silently, I asked the Lord for permission to pray that this man "lose his high" so I could talk rationally with him. Sensing His answer, I prayed out loud that God would take this man's high from him. God sobered him and let me begin to intervene in his drug abuse problems. He moved out of Norfolk, but a year later, he dropped by Brenda's apartment. He told her that he was straight and not using crack anymore. He said to her, "Tell Mike thanks for saving my life."

God faithfully changed hearts of other persons in Huntersville who eventually became the Urban Community Church of Norfolk. The same winter when Brenda accepted Christ, I met Linwood at the gym in Huntersville. He was a strong twenty-one-year-old young man who held custody of his four nephews and a niece. When I introduced our ministry to him, Linwood's eyes got big, and he froze in his tracks. Later, he confided that he thought I was an angel sent by God in answer to his prayers for help.

Linwood, one of several former football players, sold drugs in the cocaine court of the Village. He kept a big operation going with his sister and brother-in-law, a heroine addict. As Linwood drove to their apartment one day, a friend flagged him over unexpectedly, and they talked for a while. During this time, the police raided his apartment and arrested his sister and brother-in-law; the same drug bust that I witnessed while praying at the stoplight on their street corner. Linwood's absence spared him. Instead, the courts gave him custody of his sister's five children.

One of the boys attended our summer camp where he became uncontrollable, acting out his hurt and frustration from witnessing his parents' arrests. We did not know his circumstances and sent him home because he threatened other kids and staff members. When camp ended, Ruth

Gallagher, a UDM missionary, took a Bible to him at Linwood's apartment in the Village.

At the same time, Linwood prayed to God for help. Desperate to feed the five children, he could not receive food stamps until Social Services processed his paperwork. Linwood feared losing them. In addition, he took care of his mother who suffered from a stroke. He also tried to cope with his heroin-addicted brother who stole everything he could from the family, including Linwood's driver's license.

Kneeling before a picture of Jesus that hung on his living room wall, Linwood cried out for deliverance. He read the Bible that Miss Gallagher had brought to the apartment. When the food ran out, he prayed and soon found a bag of cocaine. He sold the drugs, certain that God had answered his request. As things got worse, he prayed, read the Bible, and then ran into me in the gym.

I invited Linwood to a high school basketball game where we watched Chris McGlone win a game. Afterward, I took him by my house and explained the gospel of Jesus Christ. Linwood shared with me about his search for God and the false teachings that prevailed on the streets. He also told me that he had a hard time picturing God as a loving father. The last memory of his father brought him terrible hurt. At age ten, Linwood saw blood running out from under his parents' door. His mother had shot and killed his dad in their bedroom.

We read in the Bible how Linwood could know God as his Father, if he would come to Him through faith in Jesus Christ. That night in my living room, Linwood renounced the false teaching of the Village and became a child of God. This relationship became obvious as God intervened in Linwood's life to cleanse and protect him as a father would a son.

In Galatians 4:7, the apostle Paul describes my feelings as I tried to follow up Linwood and the other new converts in Huntersville: "My dear children, for whom I am again in the pains of childbirth until Christ is formed in you . . . because I am perplexed about you!" God had done an awesome work of intervention. Yet the new believers were vulnerable, and the drug crisis in the neighborhood intensified and escalated into violence. How would we help them become mature in Christ and lights to their own community? We tried to take them to the Tabernacle Church, but the large, predominately white congregation intimidated them.

God faithfully provided the avenue for discipleship through a dynamic tent ministry in Huntersville. The Christian Broadcasting Network's Operation Blessing provided a large tent for nine days of evangelistic meetings during July 1990. Although I had the use of a large field in Huntersville, I intentionally placed the tent next to the Village. This location required that we run a special line from a temporary electrical pole to get power from the light across the street. I borrowed a pole from an electrician and added ten feet. I set out to install it in the only spot that would work.

Fred Storm, a young white lawyer who volunteered with us, and I attempted to dig a five-foot hole to install the temporary electrical pole. Instead, we immediately found ourselves scraping through broken bricks and pipes. The dirt at this spot covered compacted rubble from the foundations of houses that had been torn down during redevelopment. After an hour of tedious digging in a ninety-five degree heat wave, we managed to chip a hole only a few inches deep. I almost called our electrician to tell him to forget erecting a pole in this field. I could picture a deep foundation below us filled with several feet of old bricks.

This discouraged me because I went through weeks of prayerful negotiations to get zoning and electrical permits for this location.

Some people in the community began watching us as we made spectacles of ourselves. Our recent converts did not offer to help and acted quite astonished to see us digging in their neighborhood.

In my moment of frustration, Fred looked at our small hole and remarked, "I'm encouraged about our progress. How about you?" Seeing his faith, I declared that we would trust the Lord to have prepared soft soil under this hard layer. I dug until I felt exhausted. I kept repeating the theme of the devotions from our recent pastors' retreat: "Since Christ suffered in his body, arm yourself with this same attitude" (Heb. 4:1). Fred also wore out and left to find soft drinks. While he was gone, I decided to shove the post hole digger into the hole to measure our progress, and I noticed slightly softer dirt. Within minutes, I pulled up pure sand and completed the hole in a few minutes.

Over our Big Gulps, Fred and I mused at the illustration God gave to encourage our faith. I selected this tent sight because I wanted to minister as close as possible to the notorious Huntersville Village apartments. Many of its residents sold drugs or suffered in addiction to some type of drug.

In the past, when I shared my vision for ministering there, some who knew about the Village's bad reputation expressed astonishment, because they viewed it as a hardened and hopeless place. Even folks in the community wondered if they could solve such difficult problems. The top layer of the soil reminded us of the hearts of many of the residents. Hardened by anger and despair, they seemed closed from generations of broken families.

Fred and I wondered out loud if the Lord would pour out His Spirit to prepare hearts to receive Jesus and find deliverance in a community with such an imposing exterior. What if we armed ourselves to suffer and believed God to give us the power to break through generations of Satan's strongholds in these families? Would we find spiritual breakthroughs and relationships similar to finding the sand under a hard place? Could we bring adults to Christ and see God redeem entire families? Would God give us the acceptance to visit door-to-door and establish relationships here? Could I become an insider in this community? Would God take our recent converts and make their lights shine, giving a witness of hope and power to the rest in the community? Would God establish His church among people alienated by the cultural barriers in both black and white churches? Is the gospel powerful enough to accomplish all this? These questions framed my vision for the Discovery Family Crusade.

We decided to trust God for the soft soil in our spiritual ministry of the tent crusade. I also decided that the tougher the top layer, the better the victory. Establishing bridges with the unchurched drug culture became a priority in our programming for the crusade.

I got up from where we rested, walked into the community, and found new convert, Linwood, who had avoided me for two weeks. We recruited a couple of kids and raised the pole. Other new believers saw me hammering on it in the rain all afternoon. God used this spectacle to give me their support by the time I finished reinforcing the pole.

Next we faced the challenge of canvassing door-to-door in the Village to invite families to the crusade. Would God allow a breakthrough now? Although I found myself alone when it became time to go out into the community, I resolved to complete one court that afternoon. I chose a quiet section to begin canvassing, although several young men hanging around one of its apartments looked suspicious.

I rehearsed two verses to encourage my faithfulness: "The LORD is my light and my salvation; whom shall I fear? The LORD is the strength of my life; of whom shall I be afraid?" (Ps. 27:1) and "If I perish, I perish" (Esther 4:16). As I walked into the court, I passed an eight-year-old boy and asked him about coming to camp. He grabbed my sleeve and pulled me into the same apartment where the men stood. The boy's mother introduced me to about ten people who sat in her dark living room. She paid his camp fee, and I visited with the family as if I had grown up next door.

I walked out the door and ran into another mother named Pam. I gave her a gospel tract and she read its cover: Steps to Peace With God. Pam responded, "This is what I need—some peace." She left, but I rejoiced, excited by her response. As I then went door to door in this apartment court, the residents received me with unexpected good-will. I met Pam's husband, Donald, and signed up several other kids for camp before I left.

Excited by this reception, I went home and told Kim about how God gave this inroad into the community. We took our three kids and canvassed another court. Then God answered one of our prayer requests for the crusade. Our family turned the corner just in time to see our staff member, Gina Miller, handing out fliers with Brenda and our new friend, Pam. Brenda had caught the vision for inviting her community to the tent crusade. With the zeal of new believers and the toughness of the community, they invited the entire complex in the time it took me to cover two courts. Brenda enlisted Pam for us, and they continued their own visitation ministry in the neighborhood.

We named the tent ministry the Huntersville Discovery Family Crusade. God answered many prayers for an awesome and powerful first night. The Transformation Crusade, a Christian rap group, proclaimed the gospel before several hundred residents from the community. Several adults responded to the invitation. As I walked around the perimeter of the crowd, I asked people if they wanted to talk to someone about becoming saved; most responded, "Yes."

One Family Crusade meeting featured the classic gospel movie, *The Cross and the Switchblade*. During the film, a terrible storm thundered toward us from Virginia Beach, the next city east of us. We thought about sending everyone home but decided to pray that God would prevent the electrical storm from hitting our tent, its posts pointing up like lightning rods. As we prayed, the storm blasted away on our horizon for a *long* time! When the storm finally arrived at our tent meeting, Ken Watson gave the invitation at the end of the movie. I figured that the Lord had accomplished the most culturally effective outreach when He struck fear in the hearts of folks at that point. People from the community sat glued to their seats as Ken preached the gospel. In the newspaper the next day, a meteorologist said that the storm stopped suddenly over Virginia Beach, just east of us. He said that the unusual pause in the storm's movement usually occurred only once in fifty years. This night it caused nine inches of rain to flood our neighboring city.

In God's timing, we had scheduled our tent crusade during the time when the Hampton Roads United Christians had organized white and black pastors to pray for racial reconciliation and revival. They scheduled one of their prayer meetings under our tent, and forty pastors prayed for Huntersville all morning.

The most lasting ministry of the crusade started as a three-day Bible class taught by Ken Watson during the mornings. Ten adults studied 1 John, which set the stage for establishing an ongoing class in Brenda's home. This ministry eventually became our Family Bible Institute. Brenda and Pam attended the Bible classes and found grace to dedicate themselves to Christ. God delivered Brenda from her cigarette and pot smoking habits, and she opened her home for our weekly classes.

During the first week of the crusade, God strengthened all the new converts, except Linwood and another couple who stayed away. I prayed hard that God would work miraculously to revive them as well. On the Sunday morning of our second week, I received an early call from this couple asking for help in a crisis. By that evening, God broke through Satan's stronghold in their lives. Linwood remained the one missing in our new convert miracle. The next morning, I prayed alone under the tent, asking the Lord to somehow return him to discipleship. During this time, Linwood walked up and sat down. He committed to break off a destructive friendship that kept him away from our fellowship. He rededicated himself to Christ, to read the Scriptures at the tent meeting, and to attend Bible classes. The Lord made a way for us to get permission to baptize six adults and a teenager in the neighborhood swimming pool the last night of the Family Crusade. The Discovery Family Crusade ended with a Sunday evening worship service for area churches. Ken Watson preached on the Crusade's theme, "Being Saved is a Family Thing."

# CHAPTER 11

# Competing Conspiracies

In the summer of 1997, I sat alone in an empty gym in Cocoa Beach, Florida, trying to cope with the stress of coaching in the U11 AAU National Basketball Championship Tournament. I had arrived early to this venue with my boy's AAU basketball team for a game that might qualify us to compete in the winner's bracket of the AAU National Championship. At this midpoint of the national tournament, I felt exhausted. If we won the game, then we would qualify for the "Sweet 16" bracket. We needed five straight wins against the best teams in the country to become national champions.

Unfortunately, we lost badly in one of the qualifying games and now faced the team that eliminated us the summer before. The director of the tournament had just told me that he picked our next opponent to win the championship. I felt discouraged because I saw my players losing hope for advancing any further in the tournament.

Since we came early for our game, I found a spot to get alone and pray for strength. I told the Lord that I felt burnt out and had nothing left to give. I asked for God's help. A clear response from the Lord surprised me. I somehow heard words that I remember clearly, burning inside my heart, "I will not only answer your prayer for help, but I will also give you the national championship." I responded, "What?" I jumped up and walked around a hallway that surrounded the field house. I said, "Lord, is this You or my imagination? What did You say?" Just then I heard something like this: "I said, (pause) I will give you the national tournament because I appreciate what you are doing for young people." Stunned, I whispered, "Lord, I receive this."

When I met with my team before our warm ups, I told them to huddle together for prayer. I looked at my best player. He had already given up, and he looked away when the rest bowed for prayer. Before our team went out on the floor to start the game, I told the five starters to begin fast and jump on the other team right away.

We promptly fell behind 11–0 in the first two minutes of the first quarter. I called time out and remarked that this was not the fast start that I had in mind. I took my best player out of the game, who looked totally dejected. I cannot fully describe what happened in the rest of the half. Our team suddenly played under an anointing that I had not seen before or since. We dominated the other team. At half time, I told the team one thing: "The Lord is answering our prayers." Encouraged, my best player and the entire team excelled. We finished with eighty-five points, a score almost unheard of for this age and the shorter length of our games. In the second half, a referee ran from the far end of basketball court to charge me with a technical foul, my first in AAU, and unprovoked. The referee also enforced a rule that required me to sit down the remainder of the game. The crowd cheered so loudly that none of my players could hear me give instructions from the bench. The Lord said at that moment, "Now you have to give this to Me." Our team prayed through five games and became National AAU Champions.

I believe the Lord rewarded me for intervening in the plight of young people in the Huntersville Village in the decade preceding this national tournament. Although the tent crusade started a breakthrough for our discipleship with adults, the situation in the Village got worse before it improved. We were about to witness what happens when the Lord sanctifies an entire neighborhood.

The tent crusade had its difficult moments, but for the next few months, the spiritual battle in the Village became fierce. God began pouring out His wrath on the young men in the neighborhood's drug conspiracy. The police began raiding the drug courts regularly. As described in the street lingo, they would arrive "six deep," three officers in the car's front seat, three in the back. God spared me from being in the neighborhood during the raids. Once they screeched into my parking space just as I pulled out. Another time I sat quietly in Linwood's apartment during their sweep. They also sent undercover officers to buy drugs from the young men and then indicted them during grand jury sessions each Wednesday. This made the neighborhood quiet on Thursdays, as the drug dealers waited out the day to find out who had inadvertently sold to undercover police officers.

The big dealers did not feel threatened by this process because most did not handle or sell drugs on the street. The neighborhood's business executives, they recruited and managed their personnel, maintained their distribution system, and collected the money. Some operated so stealthily that they did not move when the police raided the courts. But I heard about instances when the police handed out their own retribution on the some of the most notorious drug dealers. Tito told me that one dealer would run from them for fear of getting beaten.

The most serious law enforcement activity occurred in the Village when it seemed to the young people that the police had given up and stopped their drug raids. Many young men demonstrated destructive self-confidence, believing that their sophisticated system of drug distribution had triumphed. They felt a false sense of security in their power to rule their streets under their own code of order. In reality, just the opposite proved true. Instead, the raids by local police diminished because the FBI had begun its surveillance of the neighborhood.

The young men who sold drugs were not the hardened criminals that one might want to picture in this situation. Most participated as fun-loving kids who joined in criminal activities that became much more serious than they had anticipated. What started as a group of friends making easy money for basketball shoes became a drug gang in an extremely violent business. God gave them over to their fatal confidence in their gang's ability to break the law without suffering negative consequences. As we met for Bible study and fervent prayer in Brenda's apartment, the neighborhood erupted in violence.

This violence seemed to escalate when the teenage gang members began picking on addicts who roamed the neighborhood seeking drugs. The young drug dealers despised the addicts who bought from them. Though they wanted to sell to them, they ridiculed the addicts as despicable "fiends" who deserved the consequences of their behavior. Their prejudice helped the youths rationalize their destructive trade. They justified taking food and rent money from people who would steal from their own families for drugs. Sometimes, the kids beat up the addicts or sold them wax to humiliate them. When the addicts retaliated, the Huntersville Posse became more involved in violent incidents. Several shootings occurred, and one of them murdered a young man who bought drugs.

The 1990 Labor Day Greek Fest Riot by black young adults at Virginia Beach's resort strip made the Village extremely dangerous for white people. Through fraternity networking and word of mouth advertising, black college students decided to make Virginia Beach their "Fort Lauderdale" vacation experience. When the students felt unwanted and discriminated against, they threatened to protest. Thousands of teenagers and young adults from black neighborhoods in Hampton Roads poured into the resort strip. I went with Gina, Brenda, and Pam. We shared the gospel with students until about eleven o'clock and then left. After midnight, a dangerous riot occurred.

I heard from Huntersville young people that a number of them joined in the looting of the beach storefronts. The racial hatred in the neighborhood became more intense following the riot. The gang vowed among themselves to not allow white people in the Village. Several young people told me of an incident when the gang beat a white man who came there to buy drugs. The drug dealers stomped on his head and dragged him into the middle of a busy highway where they left him in traffic. In another instance, a white Navy man was hospitalized for months after they shot him in the leg for bringing a food basket to an elderly woman in the Village. Before they shot him, the young people told him that they did not let white men in there.

This violence added to the arguments and fighting that occurred between the kids themselves. Noise from fights disturbed our Bible classes. During one prayer meeting, a young adult fought one of the teenage gang members behind Brenda's apartment. After their fight broke up, the older man went home and armed himself with a knife. He returned and cut the teenager across the back.

On my way to my car after the prayer meeting, I walked up on the teenagers as they carried out an act of revenge for the knife fight. A teen, whom I knew well, stood on the hood of a car belonging to the man who attacked their friend. The teenager stomped in the windshield with his foot. Chris McGlone and several other kids smashed in the car's other windows with a pothole cover. In a wild frenzy, they continued their vandalism, even though they noticed me. After everyone sobered, they all made up, and the knife attacker bought himself a new car, reportedly with drug money.

Chris began gang-related activities. Until this time, his ambition to play college basketball prevented his involvement in selling drugs. But his dreams frustrated him when his middle school held him back, and he later became academically ineligible during his first season in high school. Chris stopped attending classes when he could no longer play basketball. His mom allowed a man to move into their apartment that Chris did not like. As a result, Chris began living in the Village with his close friend Tito, who gave him expensive clothes. About this time, Chris's girlfriend became pregnant. He experimented with selling drugs when he needed money.

Remarkably, God gave me open access to Chris and these young people. I also helped several of the addicted adults to whom they sold drugs. In the dealers' new code of ethics, most considered me righteous and respected me, even though they knew that I stood against drugs. Having previously coached many of them in basketball helped my acceptance. Some had also enjoyed our camps, visited the Discovery Center, or heard me witness for Christ at the tent. Key people, like Brenda, Tito, and Linwood, also broke the ice for me. Although I learned to be afraid of the addicts who visited the neighborhood, I never feared these young people.

Sometimes, older drug dealers from outside the neighborhood sent someone to investigate my reason for visiting the Village. I made it clear that I was in there to introduce people to Jesus Christ. They watched me carry a Bible while I repeatedly visited the same crack addicts to whom they sold drugs.

I began my own kind of conspiracy to compete with the drug dealers for the allegiance of the Village's children. I saw them effectively develop new leaders for their illegal trade. The older drug dealers recruited young teenagers to do simple tasks and then pulled them up into higher positions of leadership. The conspiracy expanded as they promoted the younger people in the drug trade. When the police or violence reduced their ranks, new leaders quickly replaced the dead or incarcerated. This recruitment process proved lucrative for those at the top of the drug conspiracy. It made them richer as the personal operations of the new recruits increased. Greed fueled the whole scheme, along with the false vision of hope that the leaders sold to the teenagers.

On my own initiative, I determined to cut off the source of future drug leaders at the neighborhood's roots. I implemented a strategy to recruit every child possible into year-round athletic programs and instill in them the conviction that selling drugs was morally wrong. That meant that I began competing with the drug dealers for the allegiance of the next generation. I assumed correctly that an inevitable crackdown would end the open-air drug selling, if the younger kids refused the opportunity to be involved. I dedicated myself to preventing the recruitment of children into drugs to make this transfer of drug leadership impossible. I hoped that the open drug trade would end when young people refused to perpetrate the conspiracy.

A drug dealer made me a personal offer that motivated me to make this vision a reality. It came from a young man whom the FBI eventually designated as the kingpin of the Village's drug conspiracy. He promised to give me enough cash to buy all the football equipment I wanted, if I let him become the head coach of one of our teams. He had organized a team but could not buy the equipment because he feared facing an IRS investigation for tax evasion. He needed me to purchase football equipment for him with his drug cash.

I acted like I did not understand the drug dealer's offer. Instead, I left and began to recruit my own tackle football team, even though I had no experience in playing or coaching organized football. My first obstacle was to find $2,000 to purchase football equipment. Whereas the kingpin drug dealer had offered easy cash, I worked hard to beg for small donations from legitimate sources. Curt Kenney, a fundraiser for InterVarsity Christian Fellowship in Greensboro, North Carolina, became my tutor and support in this mission. The Optimist Club provided the helmets, and several individuals gave enough to provide half the needed amount. When I heard drug dealers organizing the same kids for their own team, I went to the sports store and bought the football equipment by charging $1,000 on my credit card. I left for a week of vacation, planning to start football practice when I returned.

Unbeknownst to me, in my absence, the kingpin drug dealer convinced the recreation center staff to allow him to have all my football gear for his team. He conducted practices each day and assigned positions to the children. A good football coach and former player, he implemented plays in his first week. This young man confirmed in the children's minds that he was their hero.

Some people talk about how hard it is to come back to work after vacation. I faced quite a shock when I walked into the recreation center after my week off. The children broke the news to me, elated by the drug dealer's coaching. I asked them for his practice time. The kids told me six o'clock that evening. I ordered them to be on the field at four o'clock for my practice. When they objected, I said very directly, "If you want to play football, be here at four, period!"

I figured that my announcement landed me in big trouble. I clearly understood the danger of disrespecting someone in front of his peers or neighborhood. My predicament had all the ingredients of an explosive situation. I also worried that a few wild young kids living in the Village might respond violently upon hearing that I rejected their hero's offer to coach football. I may have overreacted in this concern, but two children had already shot guns at the recreation center when staff persons sent them out for misbehaving. I became nervous that one of them would retaliate when they heard that I fired their hero. I prayed hard that God would distract the drug dealer from coming out to the practice. I knew for certain that if he showed up to coach I would refuse to let him participate.

Before the practice, I received a phone call from Curt Kenny in Greensboro. In 1981, he became involved in our ministry when his wife, Trudy, volunteered them to cook at one of my summer camp programs. Like a second father to me, Curt spent a lot of time raising money for my ministry.

He called to see how I was doing. Stretched out on the couch in my living room, I responded very seriously. I said, "Not so good. I might get killed over the football equipment that I just bought." After encouraging me, Curt prayed over the phone for my safety.

I suffered emotionally during our hard first practice. Alone on a big, bumpy field, several hundred yards from the safety of the recreation center, I knew nothing about coaching football. Even the preliminaries of getting the team to do football-type warm-up exercises seemed impossible. Not knowing any skills to teach, I looked at the novice linemen and said, "You guys know what the line is supposed to do. Block somebody!" I could not come up with any more techniques for them. A high school coach gave me some offensive plays and showed me where to line up the defense. Since I lacked the know-how for teaching kids to make contact, the team did not tackle well. Other coaches in the city did not appreciate a new team competing for players. Two opposing coaches even came to our field and recruited my kids while they practiced with me.

The players and I expected the drug dealer to show up. They kept asking for him. I prayed constantly that he would not come and force a confrontation. It also crossed my mind that he might send someone else out to run me off the field. Halfway through the practice I knelt down and pleaded for God to send me someone to help me coach the team. When I gave several players a ride home in my beat-up, rusty, old van, an expensive new sports car darted around us. The players instantly recognized their drug-dealing idol. Spotting him excited them, but scared me, since I thought that he intentionally passed me as he followed us through the neighborhood.

I rode home pleading for God to distract this young man so that he would not come to my practices. Two weeks later, Norfolk police charged him with the murder of a young man who had disrespected him in a bar. He became defiant and careless after making bail. When a police officer made a routine visit to his mother's apartment, the drug dealer's brother let the officer in. He noticed guns lying around and, in their kitchen, big pots and a large quantity of baking soda, the additive used to turn cocaine into crack. The police obtained a search warrant, found the cocaine, and arrested the drug dealer.

The FBI came forth with the results of its own investigation and made sixty indictments in federal court against him and nine others in the Village. The agents successfully worked the case so the dealers incriminated themselves and each other. In the end, the drug dealer and three others received life sentences without parole in federal prison for conspiracy. Ironically, his aunt arranged for me to visit him in jail prior to his sentencing. I prayed with him and encouraged him to turn to Jesus Christ. Although I knew in my mind that he destroyed many people, I still lamented that we lost such a dynamic young leader. Rumors began to circulate in Huntersville that the FBI threatened to make a second round of indictments. The rest of the dealers scattered, which ended their open-air drug selling.

With this opening for ministry, my family and Gina followed up the tent Bible study with a weekly Bible class and individual discipleship. Gina and Kim met with Brenda and Pam, and I worked with several men who tried to kick drug addiction. Our Bible class grew as Brenda's sister, Shell, and two of her brothers accepted Christ. We started in the book of Genesis and diligently worked our way through the Old Testament, exalting Christ and teaching practical principles for Christian living. They demonstrated hunger for the Word by expressing disappointment when I stopped each class after two hours of teaching. With these few new converts, it became clear that God wanted us to plant a church in the Village.

I decided that we would structure the church strategically, so that the residents would be equipped to evangelize their own community. We began organizing the Huntersville Congregation around a cell-group idea that I had learned about in a Ralph Neighbour Touch Ministries seminar. When we expanded to other neighborhoods, we renamed this fellowship the Urban Community Church of Norfolk. Gina and I experimented with each detail of the church's implementation. After a year of frustrating trial and error, we received a book just published by Ralph Neighbour, *Where Do We Go From Here?*. It amazed me that the author came to the same conclusions and methods that we also painstakingly discovered. I decided to adopt the Touch Ministries cell church planting strategy for our work in the inner city. That is where Chris McGlone's death made its impact on our vision.

After I saw Chris smashing the car windows, I called Brenda, and we went to visit his mother. We reported to her what I had witnessed and voiced our opinion that Chris lived in the Village to avoid being home while she slept with a man. We challenged her to repent of immorality and put her home in order. The last thing I told her was that I feared for Chris's life. I told her point blank that I thought Chris was going to get killed if he remained in the Village. He died from a bullet in his heart one month later.

CHAPTER 12

# It Wasn't Suppose to Happen Like This

**Man charged with murder of high school student**

Police on Tuesday charged a 19-year-old Norfolk man with shooting to death a Booker T. Washington High School student on Sept. 28.

The suspect, Derek Ward, of the 900 block of E. Princess Anne Road, was arrested at 9 a.m. Tuesday and charged with murder and use of a firearm during a felony, police said.

At 3:35 p.m. on Sept. 28, Christopher McGlone, 17, of the 1800 block of Bower Street, was shot in the back in the 900 block of E. Princess Anne Road near the Traffic Division, police said.

He was standing outside with a group of friends, witnesses said, and was approached by a man who police said was looking for customers to buy weapons.

McGlone, a former Washington High basketball player, started running when the man reportedly drew a gun and shot.

Police did not say Wednesday whether McGlone was the intended victim or just part of a group that was running from the gunman.

*"the day spring from on high hath visited us, to give light to them that sit in darkness and in the shadow of death, to guide our feet into the way of peace . . ."*
Luke 1:78,79 (KJV)

The advent of Christ, described as the "day spring from on high," or the "rising sun coming to us from heaven" (NIV) had more meaning during the Christmas season after a young person killed Chris. The inner city, of all the dark places in our society, had certainly become the shadow of death in the Huntersville Village.

Chris's funeral acutely reminded me of this verse. The best basketball player I had coached in community league, he made a profession of faith in Christ at age thirteen while in the gymnasium. I conducted Bible studies with his family, and he even led the singing. But he took to the streets and hung out with the "fellas" at the Huntersville Village. Although a star freshman on the high school basketball team, Chris became academically ineligible and dropped out of school. He started selling drugs and beating up addicts with his friends to prove their toughness. Around this time his girlfriend became pregnant.

On September 26, 1990, at 3:35 P.M., Chris sat on an air conditioner behind the Village cocaine court when an unidentified man began shooting at the teenagers. Agitated because one of the kids sold him wax instead of crack, the addict insisted that they buy guns from him, since they had ripped him off. Chris and his friends ignored him, until the young person who sold him the wax inadvertently walked up and the addict shot his gun at him. Chris's nineteen-year-old friend returned fire in defense, shooting back at the addict by pointing the gun around the corner of the apartment. The police asserted that his own friend's bullet hit Chris in the heart, through his back, which killed him almost instantly.

After Tito called me as I was installing our new stove to celebrate Kim's birthday, I hurried to the Village and arrived soon after the ambulance left for the hospital. The police stationed themselves around the parking lot to guard the crime scene. I asked a policewoman whether the young man who had been shot was dead. She hesitated to say but quietly confided to me that Chris had died instantly. Only because of his young age, the paramedics had rushed him away in the ambulance to prevent further trouble.

I arrived at the emergency room a few minutes after the doctors informed Chris's mother of his death. When she saw me, she threw her arms around my neck in a trembling hug and repeatedly cried out, "They killed my baby!" Her next words were hard on us both. Referring to the warning that I had given to her a month before, she looked into my eyes searchingly and said, "I knew, a lesson, but not this?" Sadly, two days after Chris's death, his girlfriend, in her grief, miscarried their unborn son. The families buried him in the same casket with Chris.

Although I never met his dad before the day Chris died, I knew that he worked as a custodian at a local high school. Already evening when I arrived there from the hospital, I banged on the school's locked steel doors until someone let me in and helped me find Chris's father. I sat down on a bench next to him in a dark, empty gym hallway and informed him that his son had been killed.

The funeral exposed the hopelessness felt by these young people living in the shadow of death. After the undertakers seated the family members, no room remained in the small funeral home chapel. As it turned out, the "fellas," the guys selling dope in the Village, arrived with the family and entered last. The lack of room, even around the perimeter of the pews, forced these young men to remain standing in the center aisle directly in front of the casket.

When a minister began reading the Bible, the young men erupted in uninhibited morbid wailing, loud crying out, and screams of anguish. Those standing in the aisles began leaning on each other. Some fell to the floor. They mourned so loudly that the minister abandoned the program's schedule and eventually threatened to make some leave. The young men cried out repeatedly, "It wasn't supposed to happen like this!" Once the young people finally quieted down and became attentive, the preacher looked down this line of guys and clearly preached the gospel and warned them of God's judgment. I sat in the back of the funeral home's chapel in tears. I vowed to make Chris's life and death count for something. I asked God for the power and wisdom to do my part to stop the drug trade from destroying the children in the Village.

The Lord's hand certainly remained heavy upon these young people after the funeral. The police effectively raided the community. Worse, a gang of robbers came through the court several times, humiliating them before stealing their money and drugs. Shootings and robberies escalated.

The funeral heightened my commitment to change the community and prevent this fate from happening to the kids whom I coached. Determined to make Chris's death count for something, I asked God to help me intervene with the next generation of children who played in the Village surrounded by drugs and violence. I took three initiatives to stop the recruitment of children into the gangs: 1) I sought a means to empower mentors to address the educational needs of those who failed. 2) I began targeting potential athletes in middle school before they lost their eligibility to play sports in high school. 3) I resolved to find an avenue to recruit mentors from churches to reach the young people like Chris.

On the day of the funeral, I sensed something eerie about the Village, like an unseen conflict warred over the neighborhood. The kids walked around dazed. Behind the gymnasium, I saw the older drug dealers pushing them to drink liquor straight from the bottle to dull their pain and try to end their nightmares. From that day on, Tito refused to sleep in his bedroom, which he had shared with Chris. He chose to sleep on the floor in his mother's room.

I felt intense fear during the months that followed. One day after the funeral, I headed to the court where Chris had died. Hurt and determined, I went to confront some parents there who still put their children at risk of the same fate. On my way, I met a nine-year-old whose mother abused drugs. I offered to walk him home so I could get in to see her. As we approached the area where Chris died, I saw the drug dealer with the dreadlocks whom I knew. He stood in a tight alley that led to the drug court, talking to a beat-up-looking drug user. I heard the addict say, "I don't care, I just don't care." When the boy and I approached, I saw the addict cock a handgun. Wide-eyed and silent, the drug dealer suddenly stepped back into a porch enclosure so that a brick wall separated him and the gunman. I froze in my tracks about ten yards away, as if I had just walked up on a rattlesnake.

I directly faced both the drug dealer and the man with the gun, with a wall between them. The drug dealer said nothing, but the look in his eyes caused me to make a hard about-face. As fast as possible, I walked away in the direction that I had come, holding onto the boy, and praying that God would not let the addict shoot me in the back. I felt guilt because I kept the boy close to me for my protection, thinking that even an addict would not shoot in the direction of a child. I did not tell anyone about this incident because my relatives were already putting pressure on me to abandon the Village for my own safety.

Besides Chris, the drug trade started claiming many other lives. Most killings occurred accidentally like Chris's death, tragically involving several other young people who participated in our ministry. A young teenager named Sparkle attended camp with us every summer, accepted the Lord, and later joined our junior camp staff. Sparkle and her three young cousins died in their sleep when a young man broke into the house where she baby sat and set it on fire. He had intended to retaliate against someone whom he had fought earlier in the day. Unbeknownst to him, the girls slept upstairs while he poured gasoline in the first floor and lit the blaze that killed them.

Lil' Bob played on my basketball team but later became a prominent drug dealer. He resented his mother's boyfriend who moved into their apartment and tried to take control of the household after getting out of jail. During an argument between them, Lil' Bob went to his room and retrieved a gun. He returned to the living room and killed the man on his mother's couch.

I worked hard for years trying to help a child named Teko. I picked him up for church every Sunday. I did weekly Bible clubs in his apartment, and I took him to summer camp and swimming tryouts. The school diagnosed him as mentally retarded and placed him in special education classes. Teko grew up relating to his great-grandmother as his mother, since she raised him.

When Teko turned ten years old, his great-grandmother decided that Teko should know that an incarcerated woman who did not want him was his real mother. After hearing this, Teko became incorrigible. He concluded that he did not have to obey anyone in authority, since he lacked parents who wanted him. The courts institutionalized him until he reached adulthood. He subsequently took the blame for a murder near the Village to win the approval of his friends. Even with his mental disabilities, he received a life sentence. While incarcerated, he remained in trouble until the prison authorities put him in permanent solitary confinement. There he committed suicide by hanging himself with a sheet. Spiritually confused, Teko had tried to find acceptance in the prison by joining a racist religion. He told me that he dropped out because of his past close relationships with Mrs. Trudy Kenney and me. He could not believe the religion's teaching that all white people were devils.

## CHAPTER 13

# Making It Count

*Mike congratulates Felton Woodson after he wins the
high school district wrestling title*

After Chris's death, the early sunset during the following fall months increased my feelings of fear in the Village, since every Bible study and evening visit occurred after dark. I began to struggle with the risk of losing my own life. The young people who could no longer sell drugs began robbing people to get money for marijuana. The male strangers who crossed my path in the Village became more intimidating. I tried to guess whether they were addicts or police. I became scared for my safety, wondering what would happen to Kim and my children if someone killed me. I coped with these fears by quoting this verse over and over as I drove to the Village: "The LORD is my light and my salvation, whom shall I fear? The LORD is the strength of my life, of whom shall I be afraid?"

Violence and fear framed the context of my ministry that fall. Experiencing this darkness, even the shadow of death, made the light of Christ more precious and the hope of the message of that Christmas seem more glorious. By then God gave us an opportunity to address the educational needs of the young people who contemplated dropping out of school to join the Huntersville gang.

In contrast to the drug dealer's proposition to provide football equipment, another offer came my way from a businessman named Jim Crawford, who founded Project Light, a Christian literacy organization. He wanted to partner with Urban Discovery Ministries to create a model strategy for establishing computer-based learning centers in the inner city. We linked together to develop two pilot educational programs.

The first started as a gang-prevention project established through a demonstration grant from the Office of Juvenile Justice and Delinquency Prevention (OJJDP). In partnership with the Norfolk Recreation Department, a computer-based learning center was located in the Huntersville

Recreation Center. I chose this location to transfer the discipline achieved in athletics to the educational lives of the children. We tested and enrolled children from the recreation teams and other community contacts. I also established the Huntersville Recreation Association and served as president for eight years. We provided basketball, football, and baseball teams for hundreds of children. Eventually, I turned the Huntersville work over to UDM missionaries, Greg and Katie Johnston, who moved into the neighborhood.

The learning center program empowered mentors with the ability to know the reading and math levels of the children they served. This awareness and the program's educational software gave them opportunities to address the academic needs of kids who, like Chris, experienced the same risk of failure in middle school. In a second pilot program, we implemented an adult literacy and GED program and established learning stations at the Hunton YMCA and James Monroe Elementary School in Norfolk.

The Lord gave opportunity to complement these learning center ministries with an outreach to children and adults with learning problems. Grace Mutzabaugh, founder of the National Institute for Learning Disabilities, worked with Brenda, who struggled with her GED studies at the learning center. Their success, and the special friendship that they developed, intensified Miss Mutzabaugh's burden for training missionaries to give educational therapy in the inner city. This burden resulted in the establishment of the Park Place School.

My plan to help end the drug trade in the Village began to take shape. The Lord sent me Greg Johnston, a Navy lieutenant, and other volunteers who knew football-coaching skills. Ken Watson also returned to the area from seminary. Other former players joined us and, with more expertise, our football program took off in Huntersville. Our teams started winning, and the Pacers began to earn respect in the community leagues.

I determined to start with seven and eight-year-old boys and coach them year round through football and basketball programs to prevent their involvement in drugs and gangs. I developed a sophisticated system for teaching them basketball skills. After a few years, I placed a ten-year-old boy's team in AAU, and they advanced to the National Championship Tournament. The next year we won the U11 AAU National Championship in Cocoa Beach.

Three of the players on this team struggled with reading problems, which threatened their futures. Like Chris McGlone, they fell behind in middle school. This time the Lord provided a solution to their academic needs. My work with Grace Mutzabaugh and Trudy Kenney led us to establish the Park Place School in partnership with the National Institute for Learning Disabilities and Norfolk Christian Schools. My three players overcame their reading problems through this intervention. God used Chris McGlone's death to open the door for helping them.

The Lord also gave us opportunities to intervene with entire families. For example, while canvassing apartments in the Village, I met Rick Boone, a gifted musician. Overcoming addiction to crack at that time, he provided praise and worship for our church planting work and eventually became a pastor with the Salvation Army.

While I trained Rick in visitation evangelism, he took me to visit his aunt in a public housing neighborhood. We arrived at his aunt's apartment on a rainy evening after dark. We found her pacing the floor. Scheduled to check into a detox center later that night, she already felt the effects of crack withdrawal. She came in and out of the apartment, upset and trying to cope with her withdrawal symptoms.

Her brother, Tom Tic, who abused alcohol, and her husband, Mr. Keene, sat in the apartment. As we talked with them, suddenly the shock of a loud explosion startled and scared us. It came from outside of the apartment's open backdoor. I thought it sounded like a shotgun at point blank range, but the blast made a flash of light that lit up the area when it went off. Mr. Keene slowly closed the back door. I concluded that Satan must have tried to run us away.

I suggested that we pray. God poured out His grace on the home as I prayed. I could sense His blessing upon us. I spoke the words of the prayer, but they were not my ideas; I prayed what I felt compelled to say. I asked God to make this apartment a light to the neighborhood. I prayed for many impossible things about that apartment's witness for Christ. When I finished praying, Rick and I stared at each other. We knew the prayer gave us a special experience before the throne of God.

A month later we returned to the apartment to see how God had worked. To our surprise, we found that Rick's relatives had moved. We knocked on the door anyway and asked the new tenant about her interest in spiritual things. Although the question seemed strange to her, we wanted to ask; we were convinced that God had responded to our prayer for her place. Rick found the address of his relatives' new apartment, and we headed across town to find them.

At their new apartment, we rejoiced to find Mr. and Mrs. Keene doing well. Mrs. Keene successfully ended her drug abuse and Tom Tic stopped drinking. While we visited, the Keene's daughter entered the apartment. Mr. Keene pointed to his daughter, Veronica, a.k.a. Trolley, and asked me to pray for her. Tears rolled down Veronica's cheeks as she shared about her husband's addiction to heroin and cocaine. Only nineteen, Veronica had four children. Rick and I prayed for her and left. Outside the apartment, Rick asked me where I intended to go next. I said, "To find her husband." Rick took me to Veronica's apartment, where we met Kevin Keene, a.k.a. Poochieman. I told him that God blessed him with a good wife and challenged him turn to Jesus and become accountable to the church to end his drug abuse. Kevin agreed to meet with me and work on a program of accountability. Still, on paydays, he disappeared for the weekend and spent his paychecks on drugs.

I explained to Veronica that she enabled Kevin to continue using heroin by taking away the consequences for his behavior. The next time he left, she wrote a note and put it on the door. It told Kevin that she loved him but asked him to not come back until he stopped abusing drugs. She sat on her couch in their living room most of the night, waiting for Kevin to return from the streets. Through the thin walls and large windows, Veronica could tell when Kevin came to the door. She wept as he read the note and left. Kevin had an outstanding warrant, so he turned himself in to the police and served a thirty-day jail sentence. Upon his release, he became accountable to Ken Watson and me. Our church's small groups proved effective in providing support and accountability for him.

Without the heroin, Kevin grew into a faithful and dedicated disciple of Christ. Within a year, he began directing UDM's learning center in the public housing neighborhood where Rick and I had prayed for the Keene's apartment. It dawned on us that God did indeed answer our prayer that night by making Kevin and Trolley a miraculous witness in the community. They eventually moved to Rock Hill South Carolina to help Ken Watson establish a new church, the Rock Hill Bible Fellowship.

Before UDM sent him to South Carolina, Kevin led Denise Woodson to Christ. Denise, a single mother who disliked white people, came to UDM's learning center in her public housing neighborhood to study for her GED exam wearing tight, short shorts, and a halter-top. Once in Christ, she developed into a gifted personal evangelist. Scott and Lucy Gore, UDM missionaries who ministered in Denise's neighborhood, contributed much to her growth and discipleship.

She earned her GED and became a dedicated Bible student and witness. She eventually became the director of UDM's learning center ministries and the answer to my prayers for a godly wife for Felton Woodson, the former foster child whom I had led to Christ and mentored in high school and college.

Kevin also introduced his friend, William Joyner, to Christ while William served jail time on work release. William also struggled with crack addiction. After his commitment to Christ, he ended his relationship with a woman named Darlene. She also used drugs heavily, and they had lived together unmarried. Social Services had removed her sons, and she came close to living on the streets in her public housing neighborhood. In her desperation, Darlene decided to shoplift at a drug store so the police would arrest her and give her help in jail. As she entered the store, she met Denise. Darlene told Denise of her plan, and Denise convinced her to come to her apartment. Darlene felt so weak that Denise practically carried her home. Fortunately, Veronica drove by and put them in her van.

Denise took Darlene into her home and saturated her with the Bible. They studied the Bible together every day for several months. They called me to come and set up an accountability program to help Darlene end her drug abuse. When we met, I told Darlene that she must get a job. Although this demand shocked her because she had not worked for years, the Lord gave her employment, and she recovered from her addiction. William and Darlene eventually married in a great celebration of the grace of God. With good jobs, they received custody of her sons. William became an officer in our church and an UDM pastoral intern.

The Lord also continued to work powerfully in Brenda's family. During evangelism training with her, she suggested that we visit her brother, Alton. She considered it unlikely that he would be interested. We arrived while Alton was in the process of finishing his marijuana joint. He still invited us in, and the Lord opened his mind to receive Jesus Christ. In dire straights because of his drug abuse and unemployment, Alton lived on the second floor of a slum house. To pay the rent, he provided housing for a drug dealer who gave Alton drugs and money. Alton still fell behind six months on the rent. Alton's wife, Ann, lived in Virginia Beach with his sister, Kim, and their daughters. Ann and Kim also abused drugs.

Soon after Alton accepted Christ, I took him home from our Bible class and challenged him to put the drug dealer out of his apartment. Alton explained that he needed the dealer's money or he would face homelessness without a job. I challenged him further to believe in God and live righteously before Him. Alton agreed to confront the drug dealer that night. When the dealer came to the door, Alton asked him to move out, which he did. A year later, someone shot the drug dealer in the head, murdering him. Within three days of his stand for righteousness, the Lord gave Alton a good job. He walked four miles each day to catch the bus to work. Within months, Ann, his wife, and Kim, his sister, experienced an automobile accident. As a result, both accepted the Lord on the same day and stopped abusing drugs immediately. Alton reconciled with his wife and daughters.

Many difficult months followed as they tried to cope with the terrible conditions of the house. Their kerosene stove failed to warm them. They hung curtains everywhere to keep a few of their rooms heated. With bad credit and owing too much back rent, they remained stuck in these conditions.

During Christmas break, my wife, Kim, and I took our family to the same place where Pastor Rich Hardison and his family vacationed. Our vacations overlapped theirs by one evening. When I arrived, Rich began asking me to refer a family to live in a duplex that someone had donated. I remember thinking, "Here I am on vacation and all Rich can talk about is my work!" Little did I know that Ken Watson and Alton were praying during the same week, asking God to get Alton's family out of their house by whatever means possible.

When I returned from vacation, I felt led to drive over to check on Alton and Ann, since they had no phone. As I turned down their road, I saw fire engines. Their heater had ignited and burned up their apartment. They escaped with only their lives and the clothes on their backs. Their landlord forgave their debt, and they agreed to not sue because of the heater. Within a week, Alton and his family lived in the duplex, which turned out to be two short blocks from his bus stop.

In addition to these conversions, Ronnie and Janet McAdoo, both former basketball players at ODU, moved to Norfolk to join our evangelistic outreach to inner-city young people. Ronnie had accepted Christ through Faith Community Church. He grew up in poverty in rural North Carolina, living in a shed as a child. Ronnie always viewed basketball as his ticket out of poverty. As an ODU Hall of Fame member, he vowed that he would never live in Norfolk. As we sat on lawn chairs in his garage in suburban

Virginia Beach, I challenged Ronnie to join us in Norfolk to be a witness in the inner city. He agreed to put a "for sale by owner" sign in his yard, without listing it anywhere, to see if God wanted them to move to Norfolk. Although they expected the sale of their home to take at least a year, it sold in one week, at their asking price.

God used Ken Watson to provide leadership and Bible training for these men. At the same time, he continued his relationship with the Fellowship of Christian Athletes by speaking at camps and conferences to coaches and high school and college athletes. Invariably, persons would ask him about his church planting work. As Ken shared how our strategy targets entire families, several churches invited him to come to their communities and replicate our model of church planting. In August 1996, Ken and his family moved to Rock Hill, South Carolina to establish the Rock Hill Bible Fellowship, a church plant in partnership with Least of These Ministries. The following January, UDM sent the Keenes to join Ken in Rock Hill to establish a learning center.

I switched to coaching girls in AAU basketball when my daughter Joanna began playing and won two state championships. Through my witness to their parents, the Lord saved two couples, Edward and Terrell Heckstall and Vic and Maria Rosado, who established the Norfolk Miracles AAU girls basketball program.

CHAPTER 14

# Have You Ever Thought About Dying?

I remember sitting in the waiting room of DePaul Hospital in 1990, numb after hearing that doctors expected Pastor Gene Garrick to die soon from a blood disease. His wife, Helena, brought close friends to his room to see him, since he sustained full mental capacities until his death. Ken Watson happened to join me in the waiting room right before my turn to go into the intensive care ward. Mrs. Garrick motioned for the two of us to come in together. As we entered his room, Mrs. Garrick said, "Gene, two of your sons are here to see you." Pastor Garrick broke into a big smile as he looked at a white man and a black man whom he had mentored and supervised. I sat on the side of his bed and said, "I want you to know that you are a great blessing from God in my life." Pastor Garrick whispered, "Yes, but it is the other way around. Give Kim my love." Then Ken moved in closer and thanked Pastor Garrick for believing in him and standing behind his efforts to get biblical training. Ken broke into tears. We prayed and left, deeply impacted by this experience.

Had these two men not impacted my life and ministry, I might have left this chapter in my memory where it would not stir up controversy. For the most difficult problems in urban ministry, which seem ignored by most who address the barriers to this type of work, related more to sexual immorality than racism. For me the racial barrier fell quickly. From the very beginning, the worst persistent threat to successful ministry in this environment came from immorality and its consequences. Pastor Garrick's legacy to me included this vital truth: We discovered the remedy in repentance.

In the fall of 1980, as Kim and I participated in the Tabernacle Church's Navigator "2:7" discipleship training, we asked our fellow group members to pray for the salvation of high school young people who visited the Discovery Youth Center. Besides Nat Obey, I saw no results from the personal evangelism and weekly Bible studies that I conducted for three months.

During that time, I somehow came to know a tenth grader named Sandra. Her warm personality and sense of humor caused her to have good relationships with her class-mates, and we also became friends. Sandra made me her partner in the competitive spade card games, which drew a lot of young people into the youth center.

In November, the winter athletic seasons started. Sandra brought most of the girl basketball players to the Discov-ery Youth Center while they waited for practice after school. Quite talented in basketball, Sandra scored over a thou-sand points in her three years on the varsity team.

At that time, Sandra introduced me to her best friend. Over the next three years, these girls became close to Kim and me. They traveled to camps and FCA events with us. We played basketball on courts all over the city. They of-ten spent the night in our remodeled attic and ate at our table on many occasions. I still managed to play basketball in those days and would open the gym for Sunday after-noon games. We enjoyed a hidden strategy where I would tell unsuspecting boys who showed up that I could pick four girls and the five of us could beat them. When they took the challenge, Sandra, her friend, and two other girls would come out shooting baskets while I rebounded and defended the middle of the lane. By the time the boys took us seriously and started playing hard, we protected our lead and won the games.

Without hesitation, I shared the gospel with Sandra. I remember asking her whether she thought she would go to heaven if she should die. She said emphatically that she knew, without a doubt, that she would go to hell. Her sense of guilt amazed me. I tried to probe for reasons why she felt so strongly that God would condemn her. She looked at her friend sitting next to her as if they knew the reason why but could not tell me. I shared about the great salvation available through Jesus and how God loved them and would pardon them. Over the next several months, I encouraged Sandra to make a commitment to Jesus Christ. Although a good friend to me, she looked down and became silent when I tried to talk with her about this decision.

Unfortunately, I did not bring up the issue of repentance. I used the Evangelism Explosion Outline and the Navigator's Bridge Illustration, but I somehow missed the importance of explaining repentance in these tools, naive to what went on in her and her friend's lives.

Finally, I talked her into make a commitment to the Lord. She, in turn, convinced her friend and other girls on her team to profess Christ. They became a ready-made youth group; but their discipleship faltered. They attended FCA meetings but not church. When I opened the gym, many young people participated; but still they missed something.

Then Ken Watson joined me in ministry with repentance already established as a conviction in his life. Pastor Garrick also encouraged me to emphasize repentance when I discussed with him my evangelism efforts. As Ken and I studied under Ken Brackney's teaching and Pastor Garrick's influence, we debated and challenged each other on what the gospel of Jesus Christ encompassed. Our conclusions improved the effectiveness of our evangelism. We determined to begin our presentations of the gospel with the holiness of God. From there we stressed mankind's need for a Savior. When we challenged persons to believe in Jesus Christ, we emphasized His holy deity, His work on the cross as our Savior, and repentance.

New young people began coming to Christ and growing in discipleship through our ministries. Unfortunately, by this time, Sandra and her friend had prepared for graduation and began to move on. Although my influence on their lives started to diminish, they lobbied the class sponsor to include me in the one baccalaureate for all the schools' graduations. I read Psalm 1 during the service at the SCOPE arena. In one sentence after the reading, I challenged the graduating seniors to live righteously before God.

Almost twelve years passed, and I seldom saw either of them. Sandra played basketball in college and then found a good job in Virginia Beach. Her friend successfully served in the army and traveled from base to base around the world.

After a Bible class one Sunday evening, I went with several young adults to Taco Bell. While I ate, someone approached me and called my name. I looked up to see Sandra, except she no longer looked like the strong athlete that I had known. Sandra suffered from scleredema, a potentially fatal disease that gradually destroyed her skin, inside and outside of her body. The skin on her face, losing color in places, had drawn tight. Her disease emaciated her outward appearance, but her special inward beauty shone through as she talked. I easily felt deep compassion for her.

Sandra asked me to meet with her. We both still remembered each other's phone numbers. Obviously, she wanted me to call and help her. The men with me saw how she reached out to me and realized the seriousness of her illness. After she left, they urged me to call her.

Sandra and I met together in the Discovery Center where we had played spades years before. We sat in UDM's new boardroom. She wanted to talk about the Lord, so we went back in time and discussed why she had initially said that she would surely go to hell. Sandra confided about her homosexual relationships in high school with her friend and some other players. She also said that this behavior continued through the years with other women.

When I asked her about her boyfriend in school, she admitted that she used him to hide her homosexuality. She went on to tell me about high school, college, and adult women athletes in the area who also participated in this behavior. As we talked in the boardroom, I described again how that God loved her and wanted to forgive, but this time I included a call to repentance. She said that she understood, though she was unwilling to end her homosexual relationships, since the women in her life were her only friends. She asked me to continue praying for her.

Soon Sandra's condition put her in the hospital fighting pneumonia for months at a time. I visited with her regularly and always asked if she was ready to turn from sin to Christ. She said no but shared that a friend from her old job had been talking with her about God. At first this concerned me because Sandra seemed vulnerable and might listen to false ideas about immorality. As I prayed often for her, I committed her to the Lord's care. Later, I visited her and talked about general things. Finally, I asked her how she was "doing with the Lord." She smiled and said, "I was waiting for you to ask me. I did it. My friend from work helped me make a commitment."

After several bouts with pneumonia, Sandra recovered enough to go home. In a few weeks, I felt led to go to her and talk about the probability that her disease would take her life. One day, as I left our new headquarters in Park Place, I felt prompted to walk three blocks to Sandra's house, dropping in unannounced. It turned out that the Lord graciously brought me there for a purpose.

Sandra sat on a large made-up bed in the den. She rested on the bedspread with an oxygen tube around her face, still looking gaunt and feeble. I sat on the other side of the bed and visited with her for a while. Although fearful of hurting her feelings, I felt led to ask, "Sandra, have you ever thought about dying?"

Sandra's eyes opened wide. With much emotion, as if she was letting out something bottled up inside her, Sandra said, "Yes! All the time." She explained that she often dreamed about her funeral and witnessed her own memorial service in great detail.

The Lord gave me a special time of ministry with her. As we talked about her decision for Christ and faith in Him, we nailed down the issues of her conversion, both confident that she knew the Lord and was ready to meet Him. I asked her if she knew what happened to Christians after death. Since she did not know; I encouraged her from scripture.

Sandra then asked, "Mike, would you preach at my funeral?" I said yes but suggested that she talk about it with her mother. Though I knew her parents well, I explained that I could not just show up after her death and announce to everyone that she had asked me to speak. I closed with a wonderful time of prayer with Sandra and left.

When Sandra's mother came home that day, Sandra immediately told to her that I had visited and that she wanted me to preach at her funeral. Even though everyone expected Sandra to live much longer, two days after my visit, she went home to the Lord. Her mother's church offered to conduct the service, but her mother chose me to speak to honor Sandra's request.

On the day of the service, I went ahead of the family to the funeral home. Alone when I arrived, I found an undertaker. I introduced myself as the speaker and asked for the person leading the service. He said that the family expected me to officiate and speak. I asked for a program and decided to act like an expert, even though I had not officiated at an entire funeral service before then.

In the same funeral home chapel where Chris's service had taken place, I started the memorial service for Sandra. The program listed a solo from a woman whom I did not know. When it came time for her participation, I asked if she was present. With no one to play the piano that sat on the stage next to me, I wondered if she needed accompaniment. A young woman walked forward and joined me on the platform. She sang out beautifully, and God touched me with her songs.

The Lord anointed me to proclaim the good news of Jesus Christ during the eulogy. Without referring directly to her struggle with homosexuality, I recounted Sandra's testimony. I figured that almost everyone there knew Sandra's lifestyle and probably wondered if God would condemn her. I testified with much confidence, as I had done years before with Mr. Peoples, that Sandra lived with the Lord. With tremendous freedom, I exalted Jesus Christ before her family and friends during my message and at the gravesite. I told about Sandra's rededication to Christ and about her friend from work who had ministered to her. After the funeral, the soloist who sang so beautifully came up and hugged me. She was Sandra's friend from work who helped her repent. The Lord allowed the two people who had ministered to Sandra in her life to exalt Him at her funeral.

Her mother received a letter from Sandra's high school friend, which she had written to Sandra not knowing about her sudden death. Sandra's mother said that she could not bear to write her friend back and asked me to write her instead. In my letter to her friend, I wanted to comfort her, as I knew that she would be hurt. I told her of Sandra's repentance and encouraged her to seek Him as well. I indicated that Sandra had told me about their homosexuality. I sent the letter to her address somewhere in Korea.

I never heard back from her friend, but I prayed often for her that God would intervene in her life. While praying for her one day, I felt led to make contact with her. I jumped up, went to my computer, and sent an e-mail letter to her through the Netscape People Search. I did not receive a reply; but a few months later her sister called and said that she died in a car accident. Her mother told me about her six-year lesbian relationship with the woman who drove the car. The impact of the crash threw both from the car and killed them.

Ministering to people caught up in lifestyles of immorality remained a constant in my outreach to families. If I tried to count how many promising teenagers became pregnant or fathered a child before marriage, the number would add up to hundreds. In the nineties, I worked with teenagers whose parents had participated in immorality themselves as teenagers in the eighties.

When we began working with parents, I soon found out that many accepted immorality as normal behavior and that a stand against immorality often brought persecution. This became evident in the many talent shows that I witnessed in downtown communities. One in particular occurred at an outdoor block party. Group after group of young girls performed on the stage before hundreds of their neighbors, rocking their hips in sexually suggestive ways. A pretty ten-year-old girl, performing solo, simulated intercourse while doing the splits on stage. The audience broke out in wild applause. On another occasion, I saw the same cheers when a small boy grabbed his crotch while dancing like Michael Jackson.

I protested to one of the volunteer organizers of the program. When I asserted that it was wrong to encourage young children to dance in a sexual manner, the mother angrily insisted that their culture included this kind of dancing. After all, she had danced like that as a young person. A single parent, she considered going to clubs a valid part of her lifestyle.

In another instance, a man cursed me out, accusing me in the worst language of being a phony preacher because he believed that I tried to break up his family. This man lived with an unmarried mother whom I introduced to Christ. I challenged her to ask him to move out of her apartment, since she held the lease in her name. Although addicted to drugs and married to another woman, this man spread the word in Huntersville that I had attempted to break up his home.

Changing promiscuous attitudes toward sexual immorality became an important component of our discipleship efforts and one of our success factors. For the sake of children involved, I omit many instances when God powerfully intervened in lives to end sexually immoral relationships. As we dealt with the unspoken reality of immorality and its consequences, repentance brought real lasting changes. We addressed the issue of God's wrath on sin to make a difference.

# CHAPTER 15

# Mainstream Missionary

Oppressor! Spoken by a Jamaican, the word's sharp sting caught me off guard. My mind had drifted as I rode in a white Toyota pickup along the mountain ridges in Jamaica. Stunning tropical scenery engulfed our passage. Smoke from open fires hung in the trees along the road, highlighting the location of villages on the mountainside. The beautiful sights overwhelmed my senses as they flashed by me.

Horace Terrell, a Jamaican pastor, drove me through the Blue Mountains in the summer of 1994. As we climbed further up a two-lane road, we increased the distance between us and the Jamaica experienced by most tourists. Rural poverty and difficult living conditions escalated with our ascent.

Before I heard this allegation, I had felt plenty comfortable and excited. After all, people in Jamaica related to me as a real missionary. At home in Norfolk, Virginia, most of the people in the communities where I ministered thought of me as a basketball coach or the CEO of a small Christian nonprofit organization. Here, traveling on this mountain range with a pastor, I characterized the conventional American missionary.

This status encouraged me because foreign missions ran in my family. My parents raised me as a "world Christian." Their lives and ministries challenged me from childhood to go to the ends of the earth and preach the gospel of Jesus Christ. I had a wonderful missionary heritage. My grandparents' achievements as missionaries in Africa passed on to me a sense of personal destiny and empowerment. I grew up reading the biographies of great missionaries. I watched movies at church and in school that showed people just like me, giving up everything to minister overseas. The steady flow of missionaries who came through our home taught us world geography and cultures. In those days, my family and church understood, accepted, and valued the sacrifices required of any missionary.

The Lord provided several opportunities for me to become equipped for cross-cultural ministry. When I was a teenager, a black missionary with Child Evangelism Fellowship introduced me to ministry in African-American communities. As a result, I had worked at camps for children from low-income backgrounds and witnessed for Christ in their neighborhoods since I was twelve years old. By the time I reached Jamaica, the Lord had given me almost thirty years of cross-cultural ministry experience.

With this preparation, two college degrees, and five years of Bible institute training, I considered myself equipped for missions. For me, visiting Jamaica seemed like an opportunity to gain the ultimate blessing of fulfilling the Great Commission of Jesus Christ overseas.

"Oppressor!" I heard this accusation again! As we drove along the most rural areas, we would slow and swerve past young Jamaican men who stood or sat together on the roadside. Most had gathered near makeshift shelters or stores crudely constructed out of old boards.

From my ministry experience in the States, I knew that the potential for evangelizing these villages depended on the gospel's power in the lives' of these men. But we saw no missions teams ministering to them. Those I saw or heard about in Jamaica served women and children, or they constructed buildings while men like these watched from the roads.

We rode past two groups of men who greeted us with cold stares. They stood silently as we rode by them. When we drove far enough beyond the first group to break off our eye contact, someone yelled over my shoulder, "Oppressor!" Approaching the second group, I anticipated this happening again. After the second incident, I spun my head around to look back at the men. Who could I have possibly offended? I witnessed solidarity in their glares. I had heard resentment and hatred in the tone of the voices. These Jamaican men, the future of the villages on the mountain, angrily judged me guilty of oppression.

I did not look forward to passing them on our way back down the mountain. They knew that I had heard them; anything they said now would express defiance. Sure enough, they condemned me again. Since a pastor drove me, I obviously came as a missionary; and they let me know that they hated me for it.

I do not remember anyone teaching me racial prejudice as a young person. My exposure to racism came quite subtlety. On the other hand, I easily recall hearing reasons to fear black retaliation. While growing up, we feared the threat of violence from African-Americans. A large, wooded area separated our neighborhood from a larger African-American community. Although we played in the "woods," we carefully avoided wandering too close to the other side. Older boys had warned that black people would harm us if we went there. As long as we stayed on our street, we felt safe. We played unsupervised without other concerns. We did not fear the dark of night, snakes, tree heights, nor child molesters. No river was too deep or too wide for swimming. We did not fear guns, knives, or arrows. I lost this feeling of security when a black man attacked his white female employer with a pair of hedge shears at a nearby nursery.

Then on the mornings after the summer riots of the mid-sixties, I remember white adults expressing fears that blacks would start killing white people. In contrast, I never heard anything about civil rights or the violence by white persons toward blacks that occurred during the marches in the South. The only march that I knew about during my childhood occurred when white Christians protested the musical, *Jesus Christ, Super Star*. I also remember white Christians rejecting Martin Luther King, Jr.

During my first few years in ministry, I began learning about our nation's racial history. In addition to listening to my friend, Ken Watson, the Lord placed me under several black senior deacons who told me their personal stories about the oppression they experienced in Norfolk before the Civil Rights movement. They expressed their appreciation for Martin Luther King, Jr., and their testimonies challenged me to question segregation as I became aware of the severe and violent behavior of white people against blacks, especially during the Civil Rights movement.

The negative impact of segregation in American Christian churches, even in the great movements that affected our races, became real through the testimonies of these men. I struggled to understand how Christians could mobilize missionaries for Africa and the world, how abolitionists could protest slavery, how institutions could be built for black education, and how the civil rights movement could progress without black and white Christians dropping the racial bar to minister side by side in the name of Jesus Christ.

I considered difficult questions about Christianity's role in racial reconciliation. I wondered why most white evangelical Christians did not march for black civil rights. I lived during those marches. What kept my parents from taking me to march for the end of segregation? What effect did our silence have upon the Christian Church as a whole and our witness overseas?

Jamaican men on the mountain road made me wonder what our witness overseas might accomplish today had white evangelical Christians taken the initiative during the Civil Rights movement to end segregation and other racial injustices. Did we miss a unique opportunity to unite black and white believers and create a powerful witness for world missions? Would we, in the eyes of the Jamaican men, have atoned for centuries of white oppression, if we had dropped the racial bar and joined the black community in their struggle for equality and justice?

Did segregation in American churches hinder, prevent, discourage, or distract African-Americans from participating in world missions so that our country's "white only" missionary efforts came across as oppressive in some countries? Has it turned out that our segregated witness on some missions fields, like Jamaica, brought shame to Christ and corrupted the gospel?

# CHAPTER 16

# Ultimate Empowerment

According to Matthew 28:18–20 and Acts 1:8, followers of Jesus Christ reach their ultimate level of empowerment when personally fulfilling, in some aspect, His mission statement: "Go ye therefore, and teach all nations, baptizing them in the name of the Father, and of the Son and of the Holy Ghost: teaching them to observe all things whatsoever I have commanded you . . ." (KJV)

The insults of Jamaican men who hated missionaries changed my way of relating to my own countrymen in the inner city. Before then, I had operated on the presupposition that impoverished communities were my mission fields. Ministering in Jamaica helped me strategically see these same African-American neighborhoods as a rich source of future missionaries for home and abroad. There I embraced a true, reconciling gospel that saves and empowers eventual believers to fulfill Christ's commission. Without Christ's mission reconciling black and white Christians, the Jamaicans labeled our gospel, which seemed to authorize a "whites only" witness, the ultimate oppression that offended them.

Ken Watson and I returned from Jamaica with a new missionary vision for African-American believers. We not only saw the problems that segregated missions work had created in Jamaica, we witnessed the power of God anointing Ken and the other African-Americans, resulting in two benefits. First, Jamaicans received a powerful, united witness from the Body of Christ. The witness of the African-Americans removed objections to the gospel for all of us on the team; objections that racial segregation had promoted. Best of all, his missions team connected with unchurched Jamaican men.

Second, those who went to Jamaica returned with a stronger passion for reaching the lost here in Norfolk, a significant development for those living in low-income backgrounds. The trip not only taught them about missions, it gave them a new sense of purpose in their lives. Their experience as anointed witnesses for Christ overseas heightened their faith and vision for what God could do in their own neighborhoods. The Lord used the experience to challenge them to appreciate their communities more after seeing Jamaicans living and ministering in worse conditions of poverty. This impressed upon them their need to grow, learn, and reach out to their own neighbors with the gospel. They understood, for the first time, their calling to serve as a part of a much larger, worldwide cause that began in their own homes and cities.

After we returned to the States, Ken and I prayerfully developed UDM's GLOBE missions strategy. GLOBE stands for the George Liele Objective for Black Enterprise. We established GLOBE to give African-Americans, especially those from low-income situations, the opportunity to serve Jesus Christ in foreign missions. We raised funds to help Buff Bay Baptist Church in Jamaica build an outreach center to mobilize and accommodate missions teams. Under Pastor Vernon Allen's leadership, the church completed and dedicated the first phase of the GLOBE Center in December 1997. Felton and Denise Woodson established UDM's learning center model there in 1999.

George Liele (1750–1820), born in Virginia of slave parents, is said to be the first ordained African-American preacher and the first foreign missionary from America. When granted his freedom before the Revolutionary War, Liele ministered in Savannah, Georgia. He then became an indentured servant to the British to pay for his passage to Jamaica. There, George Liele established a Baptist church and school. Many of his church members were poor slaves. With a missionary's burden to evangelize Jamaica, he appealed to churches in England for support. Ken and I established GLOBE to empower and mobilize black missionaries who will make Liele's missions objective their first priority.

My reconciled witness with African-Americans in Jamaica provided an unexpected opportunity for me to advance the gospel in justice. I found myself with the credibility to challenge Jamaican believers to fulfill the Great Commission of Jesus Christ. The churches where we served had become so accustomed to being the mission field that they lacked any sense of obligation for world evangelism. When they observed African-American missionaries coming from backgrounds similar to theirs, the Jamaican believers saw their own potential for missions and sent a team to minister in Haiti.

I still remember sitting in the big field next to the Huntersville Center, praying with two twelve-year-old boys, Chris and Tito. Unequipped at the time to address their educational problems, I lacked the means to determine their academic needs. I did not know how to reach their parents, nor address drug abuse and immorality in their homes. I possessed no practical means to give them the sense of destiny as a world Christian. Since then, God entrusted UDM with a strategy to intervene and strengthen inner-city families through the gospel and empower them to fulfill the Great Commission of Jesus Christ, wherever they go.

In January 2000, the UDM Board of Directors set into motion a new five-year plan and church planting strategy. This plan included an updated missions statement: "To evangelize families living in the impoverished neighborhoods of Hampton Roads and other localities by planting churches that are structured to provide them with needed stability, biblical training, ministry skills, and opportunity to fulfill the Great Commission of Jesus Christ."

# Ken Watson's Testimony

## "Nigger Go Home"

Someone has said that we become the sum total of our past experiences. This proved undoubtedly true in the formulation of my first convictions about white people. By the time I reached high school, I had solidified two basic conclusions in my attitude toward them. First, never trust them, particularly white males. Second, white people set the standards and parameters for success. To make it in this world, I must live in accordance with white rules. Ironically, I experienced the freedom of forgiveness in the ministry of the gospel of Jesus Christ with white men.

My mind immediately takes me back to my second grade class at Bowling Park Elementary in 1963. My teacher asked me to stand before the class and read a news article. It described angry whites carrying signs with derogatory statements, such as Nigger Go Home, to protest against the mandatory bussing of black children to a previously all-white school. Until this point, I had never really thought about the fact that my community, church, and school were all black. The only whites that I saw on any regular basis consisted of the two insurance men who came to our area to collect monthly payments. So, at the age of seven, the whole issue of racial integration did not affect me. I certainly felt comfortable in this environment where everyone was like me. However, as I read that article, this previously non-issue became a source of pain. It dawned on me that more than just an isolated group of whites did not want black children in their school. Nigger Go Home made a statement against me; it made a statement against all blacks. Although I didn't fully understand why, I realized that my school enrolled only black children because whites wanted it that way.

Later, during that same school year, my parents informed our family, which besides me included an older brother and sister, of their plans to move us to a white neighborhood. So in 1964 we moved from our all-black apartment community to a beautiful home. In this community, I took my next steps toward acquiring a less than charitable attitude toward white males.

After some weeks, though greatly missing my old neighborhood, I began to adjust to my new surroundings. For the first time I played with white children and did so without racial incident. I experienced as much fun with them as with any other kids. However, gradually, all those with whom I played left; their families decided to move away. I remember mentioning this to my mother. Until this day I don't remember her explanation, but later on I discovered that this was the "white flight" phenomenon. Whites moved out because they did not want to live beside blacks.

As a result of this flight, many posted For Sale signs throughout the community. One day my mother tried an experiment. She called to inquire of an owner regarding his asking price for the purchase of his home. Recognizing the voice on the phone as belonging to a black person, he quoted a certain price. Then my mother waited several moments and used what she purposed to sound as a white woman's voice. In response to the same question, the price of the home dropped several thousand dollars. That message came across loud and clear: If you are black, you pay more.

Living in this new community provided me an educational experience of attending an integrated school, which none in my family had previously known. When I entered the third grade, my brother and sister already attended junior high. Their school, within walking distance, was black. I enrolled at Campostella Elementary School in a white community, also within walking distance from my home. By this time, my neighborhood had turned almost entirely black, except for a few elderly whites who probably felt too old to move and start over. However, all whites of childbearing age moved out.

This left two segregated communities in our area joined by a long wooden bridge. Since my new school was in the white neighborhood, my friends and I learned a lesson about American society on this bridge.

Not long after school began, white males stopped us on the bridge daily. Though in their mid—and late teenage years, to me, they seemed much older. They allowed the girls to pass but stopped the boys. Sometimes they delayed us for an hour, and they usually threatened us with violence. They threatened to hit us, throw us over the bridge, or sexually abuse us. Nearly always they forced us to surrender any money in our possession and subjected us to racial slurs. These times terrified me.

The white males instructed us not to tell anyone, and, apparently, all of us complied, because this continued for some time. My parents were not aware that I came home late, because they both worked. So as long as I arrived before my brother and sister, they thought things were OK. However, some brave soul finally spoke up, and this abusive behavior stopped. Black parents visited or called the school and received results. The school assigned teachers to stand on the bridge, and, for a while, police officers made sure we crossed safely. But the memory of that event never left me. The fact that it happened simply because I was black became etched in my soul.

However, to be very candid, I really enjoyed my stay at that school. All of my teachers were white females. If they held any negative attitudes toward the black students, they certainly did a remarkable job of hiding them. Not only was I happy to be there, my parents and other adults in that community thoroughly convinced me they were glad that we attended there as well.

I vividly remember my mother telling me that she wanted me in that school because there I would receive a better education and be privileged to have better resources. More importantly, I would have the opportunity to learn exactly what whites taught their children. She related to me the importance of this opportunity for demonstrating my ability to compete with whites.

This planted the seed of a whole new-world view that I began to develop: I must compete with whites and prove that I could do anything they could do. Whites became the standard of excellence, the measuring stick by which to be judged. Such thinking was not uncommon in my community, to hear the adults talk. They usually gave advice such as: "Boy, if your car breaks down, go to a white mechanic." "If you get sick, go to a white doctor." "Get a white lawyer," etc.

Having such a view of society held benefits in my experience. Even as an elementary school student, it produced a drive in me to maximize my potential. Doing well became almost a mission for me, particularly when it brought me in direct competition with whites.

For example, I sought to do well academically, not simply because I should, but to make a statement to white teachers and students. In the fifth grade, my teacher placed me in the spelling bee competition, which took place before the entire school during an assembly. One by one the judges eliminated students, until only two remained—a white student and me. As we stood there on stage for the final elimination, more than the academic exercise controlled my heart's attitude. I wanted to win in order to make a statement and earn acceptance. I won. If the other boy had been black, winning would not have mattered as much.

On another occasion, the school conducted a runoff to determine its representative in a Norfolk-wide athletic competition. Again, a white student and I competed against each other as finalists. Why he wanted to win, I don't know. But I do know that I wanted to win because he was white. I won. Yes, having such a mindset gave me an inner drive to excel. However, looking back, I can see a negative effect as well. In many ways I felt incomplete until I received the approval of whites.

Once again I listened to the echoes of my community, and though many would not admit it, they seemed to be expressing similar feelings. I remember when it was not cool to be called black. In fact, if someone did call you black, that was tantamount to starting a fight. In my community, lighter-skinned blacks typically joked and ridiculed darker blacks and made fun of their physical features. I can remember times I laughed with the group, but I really hurt on the inside. Whenever these joke sessions came along, I endured trouble, because I was generally the darkest in the group. I even remember some of my friends buying bleaching cream in an effort to make them lighter. Persons within my race perpetrated this inferiority complex, which whites had engineered for blacks.

## Black and Proud

Later, a movement began that instilled a new spirit of pride in the souls of black America. James Brown, the "Godfather of Soul," produced a hit entitled *Say It Loud. I'm Black and I Am Proud.* Blacks no longer wanted to look like whites. The Afro hairstyle became popular and the wearing of African dress was "in." In fact, lighter-skinned blacks then took no pride in the white features they possessed and many expressed hatred for the "white blood" in them.

In my late elementary school years, I began listening to radio broadcasts of the Nation of Islam. These broadcasts referred to whites as "devils." They also exposed the historical atrocities that whites had perpetuated upon black humanity. They projected being black as a privilege, not as a curse, and highlighted the historical contributions of blacks (never discussed in school). The broadcasts added to my self-esteem, but also to my growing negative view of whites, particularly men.

As a sixth-grade student in 1968, I heard that a white man shot and killed Martin L. King Jr. My teacher gave a lengthy monologue to the class, particularly to the black students. She exhorted us that none of us should judge a whole race of people because of the conduct of one of its members. As I listened to her, I knew I did not dislike her. In reality, she was the teacher that I liked the most. But the fact remained—a white man killed Dr. King.

The next year, I followed in the footsteps of my brother and sister into Campostella Jr. High School. For all practical purposes it existed as an all-black school. In fact, you probably could count the number of white students on two hands. However, many white faculty members taught at the school. Here, my bitterness crystallized even more when four incidents caused me problems.

My history instructor was a white male. I thought we had a pretty good relationship, probably for two simple reasons—he liked football and so did I. He always loved history and so did I. In elementary school, I learned very little about the history of black Americans, other than the fact that they came to the New World in 1619 on Dutch vessels. I remember vividly our fourth-grade Virginia history text's picture of George Washington, standing on the plantation with little black kids hanging around and looking admirably at him. The caption said he treated the blacks well, and they felt happy to live on the plantation.

This gave me the impression that blacks did not really do much (of course they gave their muscle power) to contribute to the American way of life. They seemed content to serve paternalistic white folks who were kind enough to provide for them.

At any rate, I looked ahead to the future chapters in our history book and noticed that upcoming pages discussed black American contributions. When the anticipated date arrived for us to enter into that chapter, the instructor did not cover the material; neither did he provide it as assigned reading. I raised my hand and questioned why he did not do so. The answer that I received really hurt me. He stated that this chapter was not important. I could not understand why he responded in such a manner. Were we not in an American history class? Although I cannot judge his heart, this is what I heard in his statement: Blacks are not important in American history; therefore, by implication, neither was I. From that day forth, I withdrew in my relationship with him. He became to me a white male that I could not trust.

However, the experience did produce a positive impact. Soon I found myself spending more and more time in the library reading about black history. I no longer depended upon him to teach me anything about my heritage.

One of my close friends during these years came from a family active in the Nation of Islam. He often challenged me concerning black history and invited me to his home many times. During these visits, he showed me films and books on black history. Soon these things became prominent subjects in my conversation with others. I encouraged my friends to read more about our people and culture.

During this time, my understanding about the plight of blacks grew tremendously. My anger grew as well when I read the mistreatment by whites that we had endured. I could not remain unaffected.

The second experience that made an impact on me during those junior high years occurred in my science class. I remember the teacher directing the class's attention to a visual display, proclaiming the validity of the evolutionary theory. A chart depicted a creature coming out of the water on to land, becoming a monkey, then a more progressive monkey, and finally a man. After his presentation, I raised my hand and called his attention to the scriptural account of the creation of man. He informed me that I could not believe the stories of the Bible as literal truth.

Once again this seemed like a broken record. A white man was trying to take away something from me. I never knew anyone who questioned the validity of the Bible. Most of the black teachers I knew sometimes quoted from the Bible and spoke about its contents in a positive light. My relationship with him changed, as had my relationship with my history teacher.

The third incident occurred as I walked home from school one day. A car, driven by a white male who appeared to be in his twenties, pulled up next to me. He asked me if I wanted summer employment and, to that idea, I gave an enthusiastic, "Yes!" He invited me to get into the car and offered to give me a ride home to discuss the matter with my parents.

While driving in the direction toward my home, he began to ask real personal questions that made me uncomfortable. Then he tried to touch me in an inappropriate way. We arrived at my street and he let me out of the car. At this point I was totally confused. He no longer talked about employment. In fact, he stated I should just forget it. Later, I realized that this guy had made a homosexual advance. He promised me one thing and really wanted to do something else.

After completing junior high school, my willingness to be close to whites reached its lowest point. I was about to leave a black junior high school and attend a predominately white high school.

Once again, I would be the first in my family to have such an educational experience. The City of Norfolk began a concentrated effort to desegregate schools. Previously, all my family members had attended the only black high school in Norfolk, Booker T. Washington High School. However, I would be bused to a new environment at the city's newest school, Lake Taylor.

I went to school with acquired hang-ups from my own past. In addition, the black adults whom I respected gave me warning that the white teachers would not genuinely care and that the coaches would only use me for my talent. These words made my first impression.

I had purposed not to trust my coaches, and I made it very clear to them that I did not. I rejected all advances of friendship and would usually give them a historical dissertation as to why I remained justified in doing so. I made it clear that I was there to play football and not to be anybody's friend. Since almost all the players on the team were white, this provided ample encouragement for me to excel. My attitude was not conducive to building a team spirit, particularly when I carried so much influence with my peers.

## Forgiveness' Freedom

I am happy to say that this situation did eventually begin to change, along with my attitude. It is a tribute of the wonderful grace of God. He used those toward whom I held bitterness to minister to my spiritual needs and, in the process, heal my angry, unforgiving heart.

As I look back, I realize that God used white Christians in some of the most crucial areas of my growth. During the spring of my ninth grade year, I came to the point where I realized my need for a saving relationship with Jesus Christ.

My conscience influenced me by convicting me of right and wrong. Although my family life was not that of a Christian home, it did create a healthy, sensitive conscience. I became bothered and fearful about what I viewed as the purposelessness of life. This attitude developed in me for years. I could not understand why God would make men and simply allow them to die. I believed there must be a greater purpose for man.

Finally, creation itself seemed to literally overwhelm me. I remember looking at the sky one night and prayerfully crying out to God: "Lord, I know You exist. No man put those stars, that moon, or the sun in space. I also know that I don't know You. If You will make a way for me to know You, I will give my life to You." I cannot express the sense of joy and assurance of the fact that God would answer that prayer. I also knew He would give me purpose. I began to praise Him in light of His future response.

Sometime later, I watched a Billy Graham Crusade on television. During the broadcast, he shared the gospel simply and clearly. There, in front of the TV, I trusted Christ, His death, burial, and resurrection as God's solution to my problems.

I had been raised in church and Sunday school; in fact, my mother required us to go with her. However, I do not remember anyone telling me how to have a saving relationship with God through Christ. But God chose to use this white male vessel, coming to me by television, to bring me to Himself.

I later attended a revival service, and, when the call came for special prayer, I went forward, unaware that I did not have to repeat this conversion for salvation. I informed the evangelist that I wanted to be a Christian. This first, public stand for Christ produced in my heart an indescribable joy. At the time, I felt I was going up to the church altar to get saved again. The evangelist called for me to say the name of Jesus three times, even though the Scriptures make it clear that the gospel is the death, burial, and resurrection of Jesus Christ (1 Cor. 15:3).

After high school graduation, I attended the University of Maryland on a football scholarship. Although a Christian for three years, I never experienced a close discipleship relationship with any Christian, black or white. One day, a white gentleman who taught a Bible study on campus invited me to attend a local church. In the months to come, God used this church to expose and root out weaknesses in my walk with the Lord.

Perhaps the most important weakness was my attitude toward the Word. I remember on one occasion listening to the pastor preach and thinking to myself, *This is really boring.* My mind turned to my home church and the freedom of expression during the worship service. I found myself longing to be there again.

Then it seemed to me that I received a challenge from the Lord. He seemed to be saying: "Why are you bored? Is the pastor preaching the Word?" It dawned on me that the Word did not excite me, only demonstrations. There I asked God for His forgiveness. Without rejecting my cultural experience, I came to accept the Word preached in any cultural form as God's method of change, growth, and victory.

During my years of discipleship in college, two white men interacted with me. God used them in unique ways in my life. Both challenged me to a point of establishing convictions on the Word of God, rather than on personal feelings. I gained a greater discipline in prayer, scripture memory, and sharing my faith.

When I held a position of disagreement with some of their viewpoints, often about matters of cultural preferences rather than biblical mandates, it created some uneasy times. In this process, we learned to grow together around the person of Christ and to not be divided.

Proverbs 27:17 states that as iron sharpens iron, so a man his friend. These were indeed times of sharpening for me. For the first time, I entered into relationships with Christian whites. Although many brought old baggage into their Christian experience, they dealt with it in the power of the Spirit. I began to come to the place where I felt I could trust.

Upon graduation, I returned to Norfolk and began serving as a probation officer. During my five years of working in the inner city, I supervised hundreds of young people. Over and over again, I heard sentiments of anger and distrust, which I had vocalized in my youth. I knew that the gospel had the power to free them from unforgiveness, which caused many to hold on to their anger toward whites.

During these years, I met a young man named Mike Fariss. Mike actively shared the gospel with black kids in the community. He ministered through the Fellowship of Christian Athletes in which I had participated during my college years. He was aggressive, not only in his ministry of proclaiming the gospel, but in his desire to establish a friendship with me as well. I sensed that he really desired for the two of us to become real friends; but frankly, I was not interested. Maybe a little bitterness still remained in me; I don't know.

Mike was unlike any of the white Christians whom I had previously met. Many had expressed concerns about the black inner city, but at the time, I knew none that became actively involved in doing anything about it. Very coincidentally (by his design), Mike would appear at the gym whenever I lifted weights there. In the process of time, we talked a lot and our hearts became joined together.

In my friendship with Mike, I found a relationship that I always wanted. Here was a white male to whom I never had to prove anything. One who communicated, not from a position or sense of superiority, but as a real brother. When together, we never thought about differences of race but were caught up in the fact that we were members of one new race in Christ. As the Lord used others, so He has even more used Mike in my walk of faith. Through him, God encouraged me to be involved in active ministry. I joined him in camp ministry, open-air meetings, evangelism, and youth discipleship. The Lord used him to expand my vision for the inner city and what role God would have me play.

One night, during one of our lengthy discussions concerning the need to reach the inner-city communities with the gospel, Mike challenged me. Rather, I think the Holy Spirit did so through him. We talked about the real need for blacks who gain upward mobility, college degrees, and good paying jobs to return to the neighborhoods as living role models.

I spoke out in full agreement to such a strategy of ministry. As a former probation officer, I knew the plight of the inner city and the need for more positive, black-male role models; not merely the super heroes of the athletic and entertainment world, but the every day responsible citizen.

This philosophy for ministry struck me personally with convicting power. The question began to nag at my conscience: Would I be willing to go? With great honesty and disappointment, I had to give the answer no. Some three years later, the Lord confronted me with this question once again. By God's grace, I willingly said yes.

If the Lord used Mike to challenge me in my personal involvement in ministry, he certainly used Pastor Gene Garrick of the Tabernacle Church of Norfolk in the area of preparation. Through my involvement with the Fellowship of Christian Athletes, the Lord called me into full-time ministry as the area director for the ministry in Tidewater. I became more keenly aware of two things. First, the inner-city community desperately needed strong, Bible-preaching, local churches. Too often, young people reached for Christ through parachurch ministry were not involved in churches that adequately discipled them to maturity.

Second, I became more aware of my own need for further training in the Word of God. Faced with a desire to attend seminary, I had a serious deficit in funds. Pastor Garrick, a local white pastor, rallied both finances and prayer support for my family and me. In May of 1989, I completed my master of divinity studies at Columbia Biblical Seminary.

My story is in no way meant to deny or negate the many contributions made by blacks in my spiritual life. Indeed, they were too numerous to mention at this time. My story presents a statement of need. No doubt many black young people still grow up developing unforgiving attitudes toward whites. Like me, they need freedom from their anger and distrust. I discovered that this must happen through the gospel and living demonstrations of the truth of 1 Peter 2:8: "We are a chosen generation . . ."—a new race of people having the same nature. Through Jesus Christ, whether black or white, we are one.

To order additional copies of

# Reconciling
## an
# Oppressor

from WinePress Publishing

Have your credit card ready and call toll free:

1-877-421-READ (7323)

or please visit the Publisher's web site at
<u>www.pleasantword.com</u>

Also available at: www.amazon.com

Printed in the United States
912000003B

9 781579 215361